ONCE UPON A TIME IN GLASGOW

ONCE UPON A TIME IN GLASGOW

The City from the Earliest Times

JOHN WATSON

Neil Wilson Publishing Ltd
303 The Pentagon Centre
36 Washington Street
GLASGOW
G3 8AZ

Tel: 0141-221-1117
Fax: 0141-221-5363
E-mail: info@nwp.co.uk
www.nwp.co.uk

A catalogue record for this book is available from the British Library.

ISBN 1-903238-60-9
Typeset in Sabon
Designed by Belstane
Printed in Finland by WS Bookwell

Dedicated to my wife, Mary.
She's earned it.

Contents

Preface

IN APRIL, 1974, the Glasgow *Evening Times* published an article in which I described a public execution which took place in the city in the year 1820.

The event was described – with the aid of much research and just a little poetic licence – through the eyes of Hawkie, a famous Glasgow worthy of the time. This was followed by two more stories of a similar nature, and being favourably received by the *Evening Times*' readership I was invited to contribute a small weekly feature dealing with aspects of Glasgow's past. The series ran for two years and was published under the heading 'Once Upon A Time'.

In this book I have drawn together a number of these stories, and in an attempt to create order from a very mixed bag they have been grouped under thematic headings: Crime and Punishment, Witchcraft, Famous Men and so on. Some of the stories are published exactly as they were in the *Evening Times*, others I have added to, or joined together, in an endeavour to give a fuller, more fluent account of the event or person involved. A few stories have not been published before.

This offering is not – and is not intended to be – a history of Glasgow. It is, rather, an attempt to give the reader some sense of the 'feel and flavour' of the city and its past. For those whose appetites have been whetted, the Glasgow Room at the Mitchell Library is full of material on the city and is the primary source of much of the information contained in these pages.

John Watson, Glasgow, 2003

Once Upon a Time ...

THE WOODEN CART containing the body of Fergus, the holy man, finally stopped on a sunlit knoll above a dark, wooded ravine through which a gentle, shimmering stream meandered.

Kentigern smiled and touched the still, pale hands of Fergus. Here Fergus would be buried, and here Kentigern would build his church – a church dedicated to the glory of God and to be known by the name given to Kentigern by all who knew him: Mungo – dear friend.

Born in Culross, Fife, Mungo had been raised to priesthood in a monastery whose inhabitants had stood in awe of the saintly boy who could pray life into a dead robin and flame into a frozen bush. Others were to witness Mungo's ability to perform wonders, as when he found the lost ring of Queen Langueth clasped in the mouth of a silver salmon from which deeds Glasgow would create her armorial crest. And so Saint Mungo built his church on the hill and began his appointed task of bringing the word of God to the unknowing and the unbelieving.

In time, his fame was to spread far beyond the tiny church and the cluster of houses, where amid a handful of miracles and a heartful of prayer, Glasgow was born.

CHAPTER 1

Hawkie – An Old Glasgow Worthy Observed

HAWKIE, Glasgow's most famous street-crier, orator, beggar and wit, stood beneath the statue of King Billy in the Trongate and surveyed the hurrying crowds with an amused and slightly cynical smile. Four men were about to be hanged – and the rush for prime viewing positions was on.

Three months before these same crowds had poured into the city to see James Wilson hanged and beheaded for treason and had declared their shock and horror at the gruesome sight. And now they were back for more: small wonder Hawkie smiled and shook his head.

Still, the situation pleased him, for the city had been too quiet these past few days and the citizens unusually subdued. But today, Wednesday 18 November, 1820, excitement and anticipation were evident on every passing face. It occurred to Hawkie that there was nothing like a public hanging to bring folk back to life!

His keen and expert eye picked out those on their first visit to the city – a never-to-be-forgotten day as they hurried past the newly opened Buchanan Street with its fine villas and orchards, and on to the Tolbooth Steeple standing like a giant finger beckoning them on.

Coloured pennants fluttering from the steeple turrets created a carnival-like atmosphere, and helped to mask the spikes on which the heads of rebels and Covenanters were once displayed to public view, their lifeless eyes staring blindly beyond the Bell o' the Brae towards the grey mass of Saint Mungo's Cathedral.

Along the Gallowgate there was a steady flow of people moving in from the East End, and Glasgow Cross became a heaving mass of humanity as this tide of incomers met a second influx of visitors moving down the High Street from the north. These folk mingled with the farmers who had gathered to buy and sell cattle on this, their traditional market day.

In front of the Tontine Hotel the London coach was preparing to leave on the journey south, and Hawkie watched as the coachman cracked his whip over the heads of the nervous horses and sent them plunging at full force along the Gallowgate, scattering farmers and weavers in angry disarray in their wake and provoking a stream of threats and curses that would accompany the coach on its four-day journey.

This was a scene that Hawkie loved, and on days like this he could almost forget his crippled leg that hung helplessly between the two crutches that he moved into action as he prepared to battle the crowds and fight his way down the Saltmarket.

All morning he had been selling copies of the 'full, true, and particular details o' the condemned men's last speech, confession, and dying declarations'. He now felt morally bound to witness the last moments of these men whose deaths were in some way, he felt, responsible for his own livelihood. Pulling his battered top hat tightly onto his head, he gripped the crutches firmly in his strong, dirty hands, and swung happily into the midst of the passing throng.

Tam Young, the city executioner, ignored the shouts and jeers behind him as he mounted the gallow steps in front of the jail and began to prepare his ropes for the task ahead. There were technical difficulties involved in the hanging of four men and he was more concerned with these than with a jeering rabble whose main concern was in seeing as much as possible of the dying struggles of the condemned men.

Only when he was satisfied that everything was properly prepared did he turn to look at the scene behind him. Across the Saltmarket and over the length and breadth of the Low Green there was a sea of faces, and it seemed impossible that there could be anyone left to carry on the everyday business of the city.

In August there had been an audience of 20,000 when he had 'thrown-off and topped' James Wilson – now there appeared to be double that number. His stern gaze swept over the colourful scene and settled on the faces of those nearest him. There were still a number of voices raised in scorn and derision, with vulgar comments being made upon the trade of executioner, but the shouting stopped and faces were averted under the steady, knowing eye of the grim hangman. For a brief moment silence hung over the scene as the man on the gallows faced the surly crowd, and Hawkie, positioned between the two, was aware of the tension and animosity in the atmosphere. Mindful of the number of Irish being hanged for various crimes at that time, he raised his voice in mock despair and cried 'Hey, Tam ... what are we goin' to do aboot these infernal Irish? They'll no' allow us tae have the honest use of our own gallows!' The crowd, Irish and Scots alike, exploded into laughter, and the tension melted in the cold winter sunshine.

At three o'clock the four men, convicted of assault and robbery upon a widow at her mansion in Crossmyloof, were brought to the gallows and, in the words of the *Glasgow Herald*, 'They were thrown-off at fifteen minutes past three and hung forty minutes. They struggled dreadfully'.

Their struggling was to no avail and they found peace only when they were laid to rest in the Gorbals burying ground. With the execution of the unfortunate Irishmen and the removal of their bodies from the gallows the crowds in the Saltmarket began to disperse, and Hawkie retired to his favourite whisky-shop in the Goosedubs where he found himself a quiet corner and proceeded to drink his way through the five shillings he had earned that day.

On his own admission it took 15 pence to get him tipsy – with 60 he could become gloriously drunk and have enough to pay for his lodgings and to purchase another supply of books to be 'cried' tomorrow. Not for the first time Hawkie blessed the day his wanderings had led him to settle in the 'dear green place' ... Glasgow.

BORN WILLIAM CAMERON, in the village of Plean, near Stirling, Hawkie's right leg had been cruelly injured while still an infant, and his early life had been spent travelling the streets and highways of Scotland and England supported by a pair of crutches, a quick tongue, and a nimble brain.

His parents had struggled to give him an education when education was for the privileged few, and at 12 years of age he had been indentured to a Bannockburn tailor. He soon found that life at a bench in a tiny room was not for him. 'I am a bird o' the open air,' he wrote to a friend. 'So I laid the whip tae mah stilt [crutch] and took the road hame.'

'The road hame' had taken him to every village, town and city in the land, and in and out of a variety of trades. Starting out as a whip-the-cat (a door-to-door tailor) he progressed through toymaker, preacher, actor and schoolteacher. And was, by and large, a failure in all of them. He was at last reduced to the role of beggar and cadger and became such an expert that he felt able to declare Aberdeen as 'the maist charitable city in Scotland'. With his ability to read and his penchant for acting it was perhaps inevitable that he should become a street-crier and ballad-monger, and join the band of men who made a precarious living by selling directly to the public copies of books, pamphlets, ballads, and epic poems, issued by the printer at two pennies a dozen and sold by the street-crier at a half-penny each.

While the public were anxious enough to purchase these publications they had first of all to be persuaded that they were getting value for money. It was the task of the crier to 'sell' the story in the way that advertisers today 'sell' washing powders and breakfast cereals.

The better the story was 'cried' the more copies were sold and the more profit made. Hawkie raised the business of 'crying' to an art form, and more often then not the story he told was better than the story he sold. His exciting and vivid account of the happenings to be found in the booklet 'The Trial and Burning of Maggie Lang, the Cardonald Witch' always ensured a large audience and a tidy sale afterwards.

Among the legion of beggars and vagabonds who wandered the countryside in the early 1800s Hawkie had simply been one of many, but when in 1818 his wanderlust led him to Glasgow he automatically became one of the sights and sounds of the expanding city. He wasn't the only new arrival in Glasgow that year – there was a typhus epidemic that claimed 171 lives, and a great storm that caused much damage; the bowling green in the Candleriggs became the New Bazaar, and the Cattle Market was laid out between Duke Street and the Gallowgate; mansions were built at the western end of Carlton Place, with a white gate erected to seal the area off from the more common folk in Bridge Street.

Hawkie took up residence with the very common folk in the Flea

Barracks at the foot of the Old Wynd in the Briggait. This area, once one of the more select in the city, had fallen on bad times and the original inhabitants had moved out to the Gorbals where people of quality could still lead a life of dignity and leisure. The mansions of the departed rich had now given way to whisky-shops, brothels, and vile lodging houses.

Hawkie often told of the time when he lived in Billy Toye's hotel in the Old Wynd and of how during the night 'forty to fifty rats would step from the bed-head to my chest and from there to the floor. They became uncommonly impudent'. He also told of the young man who died in the 'hotel' and whose body was savaged by rats which had to be fought off with sticks until the body could be carried away on a 'hurley' to the Police Office.

Despite the horrors of the old Glasgow lodging houses, however, Hawkie spent the last 33 years of his life entertaining, educating, annoying and infuriating the citizens of his adopted city, where his quick tongue and fertile imagination made him the most successful street-crier of them all.

With the passing of time he became less of a street-crier and more and more of an orator and solver of the burning questions of the day. No subject was too weighty to be tackled and none too trivial to be put under close inspection, and he would be found every night in the Trongate surrounded by hundreds of eager listeners, as he expounded upon the solution to such diverse problems as the Reform Bill, papal aggression, drunken husbands and ill-bred bairns.

He became the most quoted man in Glasgow and his jokes were passed from mouth to mouth around the city and far beyond. Farmers and other country folk who poured into town on market day never missed the opportunity of crowding round the crippled figure who took great delight in upbraiding them as country bumpkins and dull fellows. To be insulted by Hawkie in this fashion was no insult – the retelling of the story would provide amusement for weeks to come and the 'victim' would be the centre of attention every time.

'Bird o' the open air' that he was, Hawkie's days and nights were spent on the streets of the city at all times and in all weather, and by 1840 his health was such that he was taken as an inmate to the Town's Hospital in Clyde Street where he spent the next 10 years of his life. It was during this time that his friend and admirer, David Robertson, a bookseller in the Trongate, persuaded Hawkie to write his autobiography. He especially asked Hawkie to record his most popular orations and harangues to the public, but received the reply – 'As for what has taken place between me and my congregation in the street, I am, in general, drunk when they happen, and do not commit them to memory.'

Despite this, Hawkie's story was eventually written and published under the title *The Autobiography of a Gangrel* (Gangrel being the old Scots word for vagabond).

Hawkie died on Thursday, 11 September, 1851, in the City Poorhouse, Parliamentary Road. The Glasgow Examiner announced his passing and listed his principal characteristics as 'strong powers of wit, sarcasm, and a devoted love of whisky'.

CHAPTER 2

Jamie Blue – The Battle of Harvey's Dyke

JAMIE BLUE, singer and poet, scrambled over the shattered remains of Tam Harvey's dyke just as the troop of Eniskillin Dragoons came charging along the banks of the Clyde, their sabres drawn and a battle-cry on their lips. The colliers and weavers who had just demolished the hated dyke scattered in every direction before the approaching troops: most of them headed across the open ground towards the Gallowgate, others plunged into the Clyde itself in an endeavour to escape.

Despite these frantic efforts, 30 of the men were captured by the bold Dragoons and marched to the Tolbooth at Glasgow Cross, to be held there and charged with unlawful assembly and rioting. Vast crowds followed them through the city, cheering them every step of the way, and – led on by Jamie – singing at the top of their voices the stirring words of *Scots wha hae*.

Strangers to the city would have been forgiven for thinking they were witness to the celebration of a mighty national victory over impossible odds, but they would have been astonished to learn that the reason for all the excitement was the knocking down of a wall on the banks of the river Clyde. The wall – 10ft high and four ft thick – belonged to Tam Harvey, and Tam Harvey was the most hated man in Glasgow.

A former carter from Port Dundas, he had amassed a fortune from the sale of whisky and bought for himself the mansion and grounds of West-thorn, on the north bank of the river, a mile or so from the centre of the city. A footpath, much used by the people of the city and the villages around, ran along the bank of the river and past the front of Harvey's new mansion. The daily procession of strollers enjoying the quiet and beauty of the riverside walk became a source of great irritation to Harvey, and he decided to build a dyke across the footpath and down to the river's edge.

The outraged villagers of Camlachie and Parkhead quickly demolished the wall, but Harvey replaced it just as quickly with an even bigger one. Another attack by the villagers was repulsed by armed guards and ferocious bulldogs. By then the story of 'Harvey's Dyke' had spread to every part of the city, and a number of prominent city men, concerned that Harvey's action in cutting off the footpath would be followed by others, decided to take a hand in the affair. A committee was set up to approach Harvey and ask him to remove his dyke, allowing the citizens their age-old right of access to the river banks.

Harvey replied to this request by buying cart loads of broken glass and spreading it – not only along the banks of the river – but into the shallow reaches of the water itself, to prevent children from paddling on hot, summer days. This was, of course, too much to bear, and a great crowd of weavers and colliers, armed with pickaxes and sledgehammers, marched through the streets and down to the detested wall. Harvey's guards and dogs were quickly put to flight, and the work of levelling the dyke was watched and encouraged by a cheering, singing throng.

The Dragoons, alerted by the worried authorities, arrived almost as the last stone was toppled and smashed. The 30 men charged with destroying the dyke were sentenced to six months imprisonment and only just escaped transportation to the colonies. The committee then decided to take Harvey to law and to fight their case through the courts. Money was raised by the staging of concerts, lectures and exhibitions, while collection boxes were placed at strategic positions around the city.

Everyone was exhorted to contribute to the fund 'to oil the wheels of the plea, and to make it GANG!' Harvey, meanwhile, had begun to slide downhill towards ruin and bankruptcy. Not only were his whisky shops being avoided by the drinking public, but other shops were enticing customers in by displaying signs which promised that 'None of Tam Harvey's whisky is sold in these premises'.

Coal was discovered on his property but no one would buy it because the message had gone out to one and all: 'Only Tam Harvey shall burn his fingers on this coal'. But despite these threats and actions by the public Harvey continued his single-minded defence of his 'right' to maintain his dyke, and swore that he would spend £20,000 to protect every inch of it. In the end it was to cost him every penny he had ever earned. After bitter arguments that spread over two long years a date for a trial was fixed for 13 January, 1826, in Edinburgh, where the jury found for the citizens of Glasgow and their right to use the riverside path.

When news of the decision reached Glasgow bonfires were lit, crowds of joyous citizens danced and sang in the streets, and Jamie Blue had one of the most profitable days of his life selling pamphlets which contained the 'full, true, and particular account of the great and glorious victory over Tam Harvey and his big dyke'. The event was to shine like a beacon through the gloom of 1826, when there was mass unemployment among the weavers, typhus and cholera among the citizens, and a harvest of short corn among the farmers.

It was a year the city was glad to see the back of, a year that Jamie Blue had entered with a song – and left with a sigh.

JAMIE WAS BORN near the village of Pollokshaws, and was christened James McIndoe, a name he was seldom to be known by. He began his working life as a dealer in hardware, leaches, peppers, and blue. His hands, constantly dyed by the blue whitening powder, lent him the nickname 'Blue Thumbs' which in turn led to 'Jamie Blue'. Tiring of the commercial life, Jamie took to the roads as a singer and poet, travelling between Glasgow and Paisley, singing the songs of Burns and reciting his own poetry. He was tremendously successful, earning the title of 'The Shaws Poet'. Indeed, his most popular poem was dedicated to the people of the Shaws, although it's doubtful whether they appreciated the honour.

The poem, entitled '*Queer Folks at The Shaws*' went as follows:

Who ne'er unto the Shaws has been, has surely missed a treat,
For wonders there are to be seen, which nothing else can beat.
The folks are green, it's oft been said, of that you'll find no trace,
There's seasoned wood in every head, and brass in every face.
Look smart and keep your eyes about, their tricks will make you grin,
The Barrhead coach will take you out, the folks will take you in.

Jamie took great pleasure in teasing the good people of the Shaws and never missed the opportunity of having a laugh at their expense. He often told the story of the Shaws beggar who, pretending to be deaf and dumb, went to the door of a dear old lady and held up a placard stating his afflictions. Having read the placard the lady innocently asked the beggar how long he had been deaf and dumb. 'Since birth, madam,' he replied. 'Poor fellow,' said the lady, and handed him a shilling!

Jamie Blue also told of the Shaws family who, feeling slighted at not having been asked to a neighbour's funeral, shouted from the doorway as the cortège went by: 'Never mind, we'll have a corpse of our ain, by and by, and we'll see who'll be invited then!'

Jamie eventually settled in Glasgow where he added street-crying to his other talents. He earned enough money to keep him in an almost constant alcoholic haze, and as often as not he would waken from a drunken slumber to find himself lodged once more in the Old Guard House in Montrose Street.

He became a friend and competitor of Hawkie, Glasgow's greatest street crier and orator (see chapter one, p1), and for a time they shared lodgings in the Goosedubs. Rivalry between them became so intense that a competition was decided upon to find Glasgow's 'Head Street-Crier'. It was agreed that both men would take a book of their choice and 'cry' it in the streets, the one who sold the most copies and returned with the most money was to be accepted as the best crier. He would also be entitled to a bottle of whisky from the loser.

Jamie returned on the night of the contest with 16 pennies – Hawkie had almost as many shillings! Victory was duly conceded and the whisky handed over with as brave a face as Jamie could muster in the circumstances. Hawkie, magnanimous in victory, shared the bottle with the loser, who, under the influence of his own whisky, soon dropped his sporting front and began to subject Hawkie to a torrent of abuse and invective. Hawkie bore this drink-induced onslaught with philosophical calm. Jamie always insulted him when he was drunk, but never when he was sober – which was in the morning, just before he got his clothes on!

Jamie died, a pauper, in the Govan Poor House, Eglinton Street, in the year 1837. Never again would the public enjoy the learned and humorous discourses he invariably ended with the lines:

These are scraps of Jamie Blue,
Worthy of being noted down by you.

CHAPTER 3

Blind Alick
– Glasgow's Seeing Eye

BLIND ALICK, street musician and poet, smiled as the cry of 'Blood, blood, blood!' pierced the chill morning air. Soon, he would hear the rush of feet as women and children hurried with bowl or basin to catch the precious liquid gushing from the open neck of a newly-slaughtered cow.

Fierce arguments would ensue in the struggle to obtain the blood – to be used in the making of savoury puddings – and the slaughterer would stand back and laugh at the pushing, jostling throng. In the Glasgow of 1810 few things were free, and anything that was usually had to be fought for.

The situation reminded Alick of one of his favourite poems:

'Tis a very good world that we live in,
To lend, or to spend, or to give in;
But to beg, or to borrow, or to get a man's own,
'Tis the very worst world that ever was known.

Glasgow wasn't, in fact, 'the very worst world that ever was known'. It was no worse than any other city of its time, and reflecting on the events of the previous day, Alick was inclined to the view that it was perhaps better than most.

That day had been a wonderful day indeed, the proudest day of Alick's life, and if he lived to be a hundred he would never forget the thrill of pride as he strode along the Gallowgate behind the 71st Regiment of the Highland Light Infantry, his fiddle playing in tune with the bugles and

12

drums which drew the citizens from their homes to cheer and applaud the brave lads marching off to join the armies of Lord Wellington in Spain.

Alick, who had written countless poems and stanzas in praise of Britain's military heroes and battlefield victories, finally had a personal involvement in the wars against Napoleon and the soldiers of France. His only surviving son had enlisted in the 71st, donning the tartan trews and Highland bonnet of the famous Glasgow regiment.

The enlistment had come as a tremendous surprise to Alick, for his son had never shared his own passion for all things military. He was a quiet boy, more interested in fishing the waters of the Clyde for salmon than chasing glory across foreign fields, and yet he had enrolled himself in a war that was embroiling half of Europe in carnage and destruction.

Alick's own father had been a soldier in the army of the Pretender, and if it hadn't been for the smallpox that had robbed him of his sight there is no doubt that a soldier is what Alick would have been. A son in uniform was more than he could have hoped for, and so, accompanied and guided by an elderly widow whose three sons had also enlisted in the 71st, he followed the regiment all the way to the Gallowgate Toll. There, sadly but proudly, he parted company with his beloved son. He returned to Glasgow with a jaunty step and plans for a hundred poems in praise of the mighty deeds he was sure his son was about to perform on the battlefields of Europe.

Many months were to pass before the 71st were given the opportunity of performing 'mighty deeds', but when their moment came they were not found wanting. Their time of trial and glory began in Spain, on 3 May, 1811, when the regiment was ordered to capture the village of Fuentes D'onor, strategically placed and occupied in strength by French forces under the overall command of Marshal Massena.

The 71st moved forward 'with full packs and empty bellies' under the command of Colonel Cadogan who promised his men that the village they were about to attack was 'bursting with biscuits and rum' and would be theirs for the taking that night. Colonel Cadogan led the 'awful and decisive' bayonet charge with the battle-cry that was to become famous throughout Scotland 'Forward the 71st ... chase them down the Gallowgate!'

That night the 71st bivouacked in the streets of Fuentes D'onor just as the brave Colonel had predicted. They dined, however, not on biscuits and rum, but on four ounces of bread per man. When news of the victory reached Glasgow there was tremendous jubilation and excitement and the streets began to echo with children's cries of 'Forward the 71st ... chase them down the Gallowgate!'. But if the victory had been glorious, however, it had also been costly. The final advance had been made over ground covered two and three deep in dead and wounded, and more than a third of the regiment had fallen, never to rise again.

Alick received the news of his son's death on the same day that the elderly widow was informed that her three sons had been buried together on a sun-baked Spanish plain.

ALEXANDER MCDONALD was born in Kirkoswald, Penrith, in the year 1771, and settled in Glasgow in 1790, where he was immediately christened 'Blind Alick' and was known by this name for the next 40 years. He arrived in Glasgow just as the Forth and Clyde Canal was completed, and the lands of Tradeston had begun to be feued. George Square had recently been opened, and public sewers were introduced for the first time. The 'New Town' had come into being with the opening of Wilson, Hutcheson, Brunswick and John streets. Glasgow had begun to expand!

The revolt in the American colonies had brought the tobacco trade to an end, and cotton had taken over as the staple industry of the city. Great weaving mills were operating in the villages of Calton and Anderston, where the Monteith family, driven from their lands in Aberfoyle by plundering reivers, were fast becoming one of the most prosperous families in the city. This was the Glasgow that Alick found, and although he couldn't see it he came to know it as well as any of its sighted citizens. He had taught himself to 'see' with his hearing, his sense of smell, and by his delicate sense of touch.

It is said that at an exhibition of stone figures depicting the famous characters of Burns, he asked to be taken to the statue representing *The Deil's Awa Wi' the Exciseman*. Running his fingers over Satan's stoney face he confidently declared it to be 'the very image of terror, portrayed wi' a vengeance!' Like many of the city's beggars and street people he took up lodgings in one of the 'hotels' in the Old Wynd, and there he met and married Mary McPherson, achieving thereby a degree of marital bliss unusual in such sordid surroundings. His loving wife bore him five children, only one of whom survived the ravages of childhood disease.

Over the years Alick became a familiar figure, trudging the city streets, his fiddle at the ready, and a patriotic song never far from his lips. He would compose a song 'on the spot' for son or daughter, father or mother, fitting the words to popular airs of the day. More ambitious pieces, however, would be rehearsed in a quiet square behind Hutcheson Street, where a witness described Alick's attempts to wring an original melody out of his fiddle as 'ear-piercing and brain-dementing'.

This probably accounts for Alick's oft-declared preamble to a performance: 'I am the author and composer of all that I sing – except the music.' His poetry was greatly enjoyed by the public, and people would show their appreciation by dropping coins into his gaping pockets as he stood playing and singing. Small boys would drop stones into his pockets, so that he never knew how well he had done until his pockets were turned out and the stones and coins separated.

Alick was, of course, a great favourite with the armed forces of the city, both professional and part-time. Among the unpaid warriors of the period were the Grocers' Battalion, the Canal Workers' Corp, the 700 gentlemen of the First Glasgow Sharpshooters, and a band of elderly heroes known as The Ancients – an original 'Dad's Army'! In this atmosphere Alick's talent for patriotic poems blossomed, and while every exploit abroad would be praised in song or story, he never forgot the unbloodied heroes at home.

Every parade of volunteers produced an heroic poem, although his stanza to Major Patterson was perhaps less dramatic than Alick intended:

Now appears Major Patterson,
you will say he's rather slim
But 'twill be a clever cannon ball,
for to hit the likes of him!

It was said of Alick that his countenance 'always wore an expression of contentment' and it would seem that his life was, by and large, a full and happy one. The city itself held a special place in his heart, and after he had fully absorbed the sound, the smell, and the texture of it all, he felt himself qualified to compose the following lines:

'I've travelled the world over, and many a place beside; But never saw a more beautiful city, than this on the River Clyde.'

Only Alick knew what was meant by 'and many a place beside' ... but who better to claim knowledge of other worlds than a poor, blind poet?

CHAPTER 4

Every Year for Ever
– The Glasgow Fair

THE 'HUMAN BRUTE' carefully examined the 20 dead rats lying on the table before him. Each rat was on its stomach, its snout pointing away from the stage and towards the audience who watched with intense and horrified attention. With consummate showmanship the 'Human Brute' leaned forward to straighten the tail of one of the rodents and then, satisfied that everything was as it should be, he lifted the first rat and began to skin it – with his teeth!

In the next booth a dying man lay staring up at the line of people filing past the bed on which he lay, naked except for a cloth draped across his loins. Young girls giggled, and pointed to the rib-cage threatening to burst its way through the tautly drawn skin, while an elderly woman, convinced that the bag-of-bones before her was nothing more than a corpse, prodded roughly at a naked arm. She and the girls screamed as the 'corpse' pulled its arm aside, and the owner of the booth hurried in to move them on and clear the way for others waiting their turn to see 'The Living Skeleton'.

On the other side of the Saltmarket the Penny Theatres were doing a roaring trade as a steady flow of drunken revellers, fresh from the whisky-shops of the Briggait, hurried in to join the women with whom 'every filthy joke and liberty' would be taken.

On the edge of the Common Green showmen cried of the wonders to be found behind the canvas doors of their colourful booths ... tattooed men and bearded ladies ... dancing bears and ferocious lions ... Irish giants and English dwarves ... two-headed calves and *Human Monsters a Terror to Behold!*

This was the Glasgow Fair of the mid-19th century, and scenes of drunkenness and immorality, fighting and thieving, gambling and general mischief-making, had reached the point when the city fathers could take no more. In 1870 a resolution was passed that ended the letting of the ground in front of Jail Square for the holding of the shows, and a contemporary historian was moved to remark, 'We cannot but exult at the final annihilation of the Shows at the Glasgow Fair.'

That it was to be the end of the shows held in the Saltmarket there can be no doubt, but the 'final annihilation'? It would take more than a town council resolution to end the merry-making begun nearly 700 years earlier when King William the Lion granted Bishop Jocelyn the right to hold a fair 'to be kept at Glasgow, and to be held every year for ever.'

THE HISTORY of Glasgow's July Fair is almost a history of the city itself. Begun in the year 1190 the Fair was held on a plot of land west of the High Street and behind what is now George Street for hundreds of years. It was the custom then to begin the Fair on the octaves of the Apostles Peter and Paul, 6 July, and for eight days after.

These early Fairs were quiet, rural gatherings, with the sale and barter of fruit and vegetables, pots and pans, earthenware and hand-woven clothing. There would be music and dancing for the adults, games and amusements for the children. But with the gradual expansion of the population, the Fair began to lose its peaceful, idyllic atmosphere, and by 1574 it was seen fit to ordain that every booth-holder should be armed with 'battleaxe, coat-of-mail, and steel bonnet' so as to assist in quelling any disturbance that might arise. As a further precaution and aid to peace, citizens were ordered to 'take off their accustomed armour' during the period of the Fair.

The fact that a Sunday was included within the eight days of the Fair became such a source of annoyance to traders and public alike in 1744 it was decided that the date of the Fair would be changed. The city magistrates resolved that 'as the Sabbath stops and interrupts the course of the Fair' it should then begin on the first Monday of July and end on the following Saturday. Eight years later changes in the calendar created a period of angry confusion as to when the Fair did or did not begin. At last it came to be accepted that the second Monday of July was the day when Glasgow would begin the annual week of trade and festivities.

By the turn of that century the shows had moved to the Common Green in front of Jail Square, now named Jocelyn Square (after the Bishop who started it all). Every July travelling shows from all over the country would converge upon the Saltmarket, turning the area into a 'shocking Babel of noise' from which the more respectable and wealthy citizens fled in horror, leaving Glasgow in the hands of the poorer classes who were as yet unable to afford the luxury of holidays away from the city.

In 1815 the city fathers decided to turn the situation to some profit and began to let the Common Green to the showmen, and by 1870 this annual levy had swollen to the then not inconsiderable sum of £590 3s 10d. It was therefore with the greatest reluctance that the keepers of the city purse gave in to public pressure and stopped the letting of the ground. The shows – 'immoral and a disgrace' were banished to Vinegar Hill on the eastern fringes of the city.

But times were changing. Holiday periods became longer, money became more plentiful and people became more adventurous. The call of the Clyde Coast became irresistible to Glaswegians and the era of mass exodus from the city during the Glasgow Fair Fortnight arrived to introduce the exotic pleasures of Rothesay, Dunoon, and Ayr to succeeding generations of Glasgow's children.

No matter how fashions change, no matter where the shows are moved to, no matter what objections may be raised by the protesters, the Shows will be there for a long time to come ... the visible, continuing link with the Fair that begun over 800 years ago, and was ordained by Royal Charter to continue 'every year for ever'.

CHAPTER 5

Riot and Civil Disturbance

WHEN THE TOWNS and villages of Scotland stood in constant danger of attack from ambitious noblemen or foreign invaders every citizen was expected to be armed and ready to repel the common enemy. This understanding was made official by an Act of Parliament of 1425, commanding all citizens to present themselves four times yearly at the 'Weaponschawings' – the showing of weapons.

On these occasions, the men of Glasgow would parade in force, armed with 'sword, speare, and dagger'. Anyone failing to attend was fined, and the money thus gathered was put towards the causewaying of the public streets.

The weaponschawings were held on the Butts, a piece of common ground spreading north and east from the Gallowgate. In 1544, the people of Glasgow were involved in a bloody conflict in which they aligned themselves with the Earl of Glencairn against the Earl of Arran, the Queen's Regent. In the Battle of the Butt's victory went to the Earl of Arran, and to show his displeasure towards the wayward Glaswegians who had opposed him the angry Regent handed the town over to his victorious and bloodthirsty army.

In the looting and pillaging that followed every moveable object of worth was taken from the terrified people, even doors and shutters were ripped from their fittings, and the only horror spared the town was that of being put to the torch.

On another, less disastrous occasion, the men of Glasgow marched out of the city to battle with rioters who had threatened to burn down the Garscube home of the county's hated Deputy Lieutenant. Scarlet tunics heaving with pride and valour, the part-time soldiers of the Royal Glasgow Volunteers clasped musket to shoulder and marched at the double towards the field of battle, determined to be there before their more famous and more glamorous rivals, the Glasgow Volunteer Cavalry. If there was glory to be won this day then the humble foot-sloggers of Glasgow were going to have it or die in the attempt!

Arriving at Garscube ahead of their arch-rivals, ready and willing to give their all, they found themselves under immediate and heavy attack from a gang of stone-throwing urchins. It was with some difficulty that the jeering, unimpressed vandals were at last sent packing, while the soldiers dug in, ready to repel the fierce onslaught about to befall them. Having left the city without food or drink in their haste to be first upon the scene, however, the onslaught they suffered from most was hunger and thirst.

A messenger eventually arrived to inform the intrepid Volunteers that their presence was no longer required. The rioters had been intercepted and put to ignominious flight – by the Cavalry! Trudging back to Glasgow the despondent Volunteers were attacked by a large and ferocious farm dog. Despite repeated attempts to shoot it the enraged and fearless beast proceeded to create havoc among the increasingly alarmed warriors. Even a determined bayonet charge was eluded, with the bayoneteers left sprawling in the mud. Their ordeal ended only when the brute tired of the sport and left to investigate another dog.

Dreams of glory lost to the barking of a dog and the clatter of cavalry hooves, the weary Volunteers left the Battle of Garscube and returned to the tranquillity and blessed comfort of the city's inns and taverns. We may be sure that whatever toasts were proposed, the health of the Glasgow Volunteer Cavalry was not one of them.

The Cavalry was out of favour on yet another occasion, this time within the confines of Glasgow's Argyll Arcade. Shoppers strolled sedately from jewellers to milliners, from toymakers to dressmakers, safe from the hustle and bustle of the workaday city streets. Or at least that's the way it was until Lieutenant Knox of the 15th Hussars, equipped with lance, sabre, and carbine, wheeled his foam-flecked charger into the Arcade and began a full-blooded gallop that left in its wake a scattered trail of astonished and terrified shoppers.

John Robertson Reid, builder of the Arcade, was more than a little upset, especially when he discovered that the ride had been made for a bet – a charge from the Cavalry Barracks in Eglinton Street and through to the far side of the Arcade in five minutes! John Robertson Reid demanded, but did not receive, an apology, and being a man of some determination he then had Lieutenant Knox summonsed before the sitting magistrate in Glasgow Police Office, where he was severely censured and fined £5, the highest sum that could be imposed under the Police Act. The Lieutenant paid the fine and left the court laughing with his Cavalry companions.

Reid, far from satisfied, and with his dander up, then appealed to his old friend Peter McKenzie, publisher of the radical weekly journal, the *Loyal Reformer's Gazette*. It was a situation tailor-made for McKenzie's crusading talents. He published a searing attack upon the Hussars, suggesting that a spell of duty on foreign soil would be a suitable punishment for the officers who had treated Glasgow's citizens with such contempt. To the shock and horror of the 15th Hussars a full regimental inquiry was instituted and held in the George Hotel on 26 October, 1838.

Both Reid and McKenzie had the satisfaction of being present when the case against Lieutenant Knox and his friends was found proven. They obtained further satisfaction from the punishment meted out to the disgraced Hussars who were banishmed from Glasgow to an immediate posting to Madras, in the East Indies. And that's probably why we don't often see armed Hussars charging through the Argyll Arcade these days.

GLASWEGIANS of old seem to have had a predeliction towards rioting. Almost any excuse was used to fill the streets with angry, shouting crowds – and if a confrontation with the military could be included then so much the better. Here are a few of the incidents which brought the city to a halt while the inhabitants took the law – and their lives – into their own hands ...

THE MALT TAX RIOT

ON 23 JUNE, 1725, the Shawfield Mansion was the most elegant and sumptuous building in Glasgow. On June 24 it was a smouldering, bloodstained shell.

Standing where Glassford Street now meets the Trongate, the mansion was the home of Daniel Campbell, MP for the city and a voter in favour of the hated Malt Tax, which had added three pennies to the price of a barrel of ale.

On the night in question, a mob of furious and drouthy citizens descended upon Campbell's mansion, destroying fabric and furnishings. They were prevented from pulling down the very walls only by the brave and timely intervention of the city magistrates.

The following day the mob attacked troops sent to defend what was left of the wrecked mansion. Nine of the rioters were killed before the soldiers were forced to flee to the safety of Dumbarton Castle. This was enough to alarm the Government, and General Wade was sent with an army to quell the unruly Glaswegians.

Nineteen people were arrested and tried for the sacking of the mansion, two of them were banished from the city forever, the others were sentenced to be flogged through the city streets.

Campbell applied to Parliament for compensation, and the city was ordered to pay him the grand sum of £9000. The money was raised by putting a tax on beer and ale!

SATURDAY NIGHT STONE BATTLE

IT WAS A DARK and sultry night in the year 1654, and an ominous slilence hung over the streets and vennels around the Old Bridge at the foot of Stockwell Street. Nothing moved ... no one was abroad ... everything was still. That is, until one looked carefully!

There were furtive figures lurking in doorways, hiding behind casks, creeping and darting ever forward towards the river's edge.

The observant watcher would also see an occasional head being raised above the piles of timber that Bailie Craig stored on the island lying in the channel of the river between the Old and New Bridges. This island, occupied in force by young men from the south of the river, was under attack by men from the north.

The traditional Saturday night stone battle between Glaswegians and Gorbalonians was about to begin!

Suddenly, a fearful cry of 'charge!' rent the air, and in a flash the lurking figures leapt screaming into view, sending a deadly hail of stones and rocks raining down upon the enemy. As the Gorbalonians covered their heads and waited for the deluge to abate a band of wily Glaswegians came charging across the shallow river – from the south!

Fierce hand-to-hand fighting then ensued as the men on the north bank rushed unopposed to the assistance of their commando colleagues. Outfought and outmanoeuvred, the Gorbalonians fled the island in bloody disarray, leaving the hated Glaswegians triumphant once more.

Just waiting till the next Saturday ...

RIOT AT 'THE HOUSE OF FEAR'

THE SATURDAY NIGHT stragglers approached the gloomy Clyde Street mansion with more than a hint of apprehension. It had been the former home of the late Bob Dragon (see p63), the ugliest man in Glasgow. It was here that he had taken his life, and here his ghost was said to walk around the house in the twilight hours. The house was now occupied by George Provand, who claimed to be an oil and colour merchant but who was reputed to be one of the city's dreaded body-snatchers. It was certainly a frightening place to be and on this particular night, dark clouds were flitting across the face of the moon and whisps of fog drifting across from the silent river.

One window of the mansion was unshuttered and here the curious gathered to stare into the dim recesses of the room, their straining eyes ready to accept any dark and dreadful secret it might contain.

What they saw was a table, dripping red, while across the floor a red smear glittered in the fitful light. On the table, half hidden by the clinging gloom, could be seen two black, rounded shapes that could surely have been nothing else but ... human heads!

With cries of terror the horrified onlookers took to their heels.

The story spread like wildfire throughout the city and as dawn broke a vast crowd gathered outside the mansion, wakening Provand with shouted threats and a hail of stones.

Mystified by the disjointed cries of 'body-snatcher', 'blood', and 'human heads', he hurried to his workroom and found it just as he had left it the night before – the red paint he had been mixing and had spilled was dried to the table and floor, and the two large jars of black paint were standing at the end of the table. So what was all the shouting about?

The enraged mob were inside Provand's house and had begun the process of destroying – or stealing – everything they could get their hands on. Furniture and bedding were thrown into the Clyde, while gold and silver objects mysteriously disappeared. The police, unable to control the mob, called out the militia, the Riot Act was read, and the ringleaders quickly rounded up.

The arrested men were sentenced to 14 years transportation to the colonies, while one of them, Richard Campbell, an ex-policeman, was singled out for special punishment. On 8 May, 1822, tied to the back of an open cart, he was publicly flogged through the city streets, the last man to be so punished in Glasgow.

LADY CHARLOTTE CAMPBELL'S LEG

THE NEWS spread through the town like wildfire: 'Lady Charlotte Campbell ... in the Trongate ... half-naked!' Half of the male population of Glasgow rushed to the scene – the other half were already there. And who could blame them? The most famous beauty of the day – half naked!

Pursued by an eye-popping mass of lusting Glaswegians, Lady Charlotte had run into a nearby shop where she begged the owner to protect her from the leering, crushing mob. The frightened shopkeeper closed his doors, put up the shutters, then made a hasty exit via the back window. In a matter of moments he was in the Candleriggs guardhouse telling a police sergeant that a terrible danger was facing her Ladyship.

Charging to the rescue, the sergeant and his troops quickly dispersed the unruly crowd then bundled their eager way into the shop to offer comfort and solace to the young Lady Charlotte. Imagine their faces when they discovered that the shocking Lady had already flown. Following the shopkeeper's example, she had scrambled through the back window and made her tearful way to the safety of the Black Bull Inn, a sadder but wiser person. Never again would she try to follow the dictates of Parisian fashion and wear a dress described by an enthusiastic witness as being 'as short as a Highlandman's philabeg [kilt]' – showing not only her pretty little ankle, but also the beautiful contour of the calf of her leg.

THE TREATY OF UNION

WHEN THE ARTICLES of the proposed Treaty of Union between Scotland and England were published in 1706, Scotland was in ferment. It seemed to the people that the independence so dearly bought and held was being surrendered, and that their free and separate nation was being reduced to a mere province.

Petitions deploring the Union were sent from every town and village in the land. The General Assembly declared a day of fast to implore divine intervention in this national calamity, while congregations were exhorted to 'be up and valiant for the city of our God'. At Glasgow Cross the Articles of Treaty were publicly burned by an angry crowd that later stormed the Tolbooth, seizing the arms stored there. The Town Guard was put to flight and the city fell into the hands of the people. A detachment of Dragoons were hurriedly sent for and the rebellion was quickly suppressed. In Edinburgh rioting mobs attacked and destroyed the home of the Lord Provost while the Scottish Parliament was passing, clause by clause, the Articles of the Treaty.

On 1 May, 1707, the Treaty of Union became law, and Scotland ceased to be an independent, sovereign nation.

CHAPTER 6

Crime and Punishment

WHEN THE BODY of Dr William Pritchard was removed from the gallows on 28 June, 1865, it was more than the end of a hanging. The era of Glasgow's public executions had also come to a close.

Since 1765, 111 men and women had been judicially killed before the horrified and fascinated eyes of the city's inhabitants. Although the place of execution had varied over the years, the method had changed little after the trap-door replaced the horsedrawn cart on which the condemned felon stood before swinging into oblivion.

In 1781 the gallows were moved from the outskirts of town to the yard of the Bishop's Palace (also known as the Castle of Glasgow) and 12 people died here. The gibbet, when not in use, was stored in the crypt of the Cathedral. Seven years later the hangman's place of work moved to Glasgow Cross where 22 criminals paid the supreme penalty society could impose.

By 1814 the public gallows had made its last flitting, and entered into its busiest period. Seventy-one executions were witnessed by countless thousands who packed the Saltmarket and fought desperately to gain the most advantageous viewpoints. Town officer William Crawford had the dubious distinction of officiating at 58 of the hangings.

Not all of Glasgow's executions went quite as planned, however, as on the occasion when murderer Andrew Marshall was taken up the High Street in an open cart to the then place of execution – on the common ground beyond the Cathedral.

Children running beside the cart beat their hands in time to the town drummer, while their elders pointed out the magistrates and town officers walking in solemn and stately procession behind.

Arriving at the gallows the hangman quickly placed a hood over the terrified prisoner's head, giving him a taste of the darkness to come. Next came the noose around his neck, and then the signal to draw the cart forward and leave Marshall dancing in the air.

As the whip cracked across the horse's flank, the condemned man, with a strength born of fear and desperation, freed his bound hands and leapt blindly upwards to grasp the gallows' arm.

The executioner, unused to such death-defying antics, could only stare open mouthed at the figure swinging above him, and it was only when the outraged city magistrates commanded him to do something that he at last sprang into action. Pulling desperately on Marshall's legs he vainly attempted to complete the execution, but it was only when a heavy stave was vigorously applied to the murderer's clutching hands that his grip was eventually broken, and his life taken.

IN 1605 the city magistrates had not one, but two, hanging problems. There was a prisoner in the Tolbooth due to be hanged for theft but there was no executioner to hang him. This problem was neatly resolved by offering the prisoner a free pardon on one condition – that he took the job of hangman.

He accepted. On one occasion the lack of a hangman made necessary the hiring of Edinburgh's executioner. This gentleman came to Glasgow and listed among his expenses two shillings for a padlock and hasp. Inquiries revealed that the padlock was required to lock up the hangman's drunken wife while he was away on 'business'.

Finding a respectable hangman became so difficult that the city fathers were eventually forced to place the following advertisement in the Glasgow Courier 'Wanted, for the City of Glasgow, an executioner. The magistrates are determined to accept none but a sober, well-behaved man.'

In 1798 a very respectable hangman was found. During the hanging of murderer John McMillan, Provost John Dunlop pushed the nervous, fumbling, official executioner aside and calmly drew the bolt himself, sending McMillan swinging to his death. From then on, he was known as 'Our Hangman, the Lord Provost'.

Not every criminal was asked to pay his debt to society on the scaffold – there were other punishments awaiting the wrongdo'er, as John McIvor and Archibald McCallum found as they stood in the pillory at Glasgow

Cross and resigned themselves to the barrage of rotten eggs, turnips and potatoes, thrown at them by a cheerful Glasgow mob.

Having been found guilty of boring holes in the good ship *Enterprise* in order to sink her and thereby defraud the underwriters, McIvor and McCallum were putting on as brave a face as possible in the rather unfortunate circumstances. It was only when a large stone hit McIvor full on the crown of the head that real apprehension set in.

Throwing stones at pilloried prisoners was simply 'not done', and the stone thrower on this occasion found himself at the receiving end of some of the vegetables meant for the two prisoners. While the sense of fair play being exhibited by the mob was all very commendable, it was also misplaced ... both McIvor and McCallum were wearing copper-lined wigs!

The mob was not always so considerate. One rather rash prisoner who had the temerity to hurl verbal abuse from the pillory found himself being seized and rushed shoulder high down the Saltmarket towards the river. Having visions of being 'dooked' in the cold waters of the Clyde he struggled desperately to free himself.

When the mob turned into Great Clyde Street and headed towards the police dung depot he struggled even more, but to no avail and the defiant (but foolish) prisoner disappeared into a mountain of malodorous horse manure.

In even earlier times the city's criminals suffered the added indignity – and tremendous pain – of being drummed out of town. Not only men, but women, too, as on the day when Tam McCluckie, preceded by the town officers, drove his horse and cart along the Trongate waving cheerfully to the crowds lining the streets and watching from the windows of their homes.

Behind him walked Mary Douglas, her hands bound together and linked to the cart by a long, loose rope. By her side strode hangman Jock Sutherland, the cat o' nine tails swinging menacingly from his large and powerful hand. Behind them both marched the town drummer, his steady, mournful beat proclaiming the fact that Mary Douglas, housebreaker and thief, was being drummed out of town. Her naked back crossed and scarred from the flogging received at Glasgow Cross, Mary stumbled along the rutted roadway with tears in her eyes, and the jeers of onlookers ringing in her ears. At Stockwell Street the cart was stopped once more while Sutherland administered another whipping on the almost fainting woman. At Jamaica Street it was repeated once more, and all the while the drummer drummed, and all the while the mob yelled happy approval. Arriving at last at the village of Anderston, the prisoner was released with the stern and solemn warning not to set foot in Glasgow ever again. A final push was enough to send her sprawling and fainting to the ground, safely beyond the city limits.

Yet another punishment – reserved almost solely for women – was on one occasion meted out to the unfortunate Janet Foreside, a talkative woman who liked nothing better than a good blether, spiced if at all possible with a juicy piece of gossip. On 25 July, 1584 the talkative Janet stood at the Tolbooth for four hours unable to utter a single word, while her hands, so often an extension of her busy tongue, lay still and pale before her. There was a simple explanation for this unusual state of affairs – her hands were manacled to the Tolbooth wall and her tongue was held in the iron grip of the branks, a bridle used to still the idle chatter of slandering and malicious women.

The unfortunate Janet was condemned to stand thus for as long as the woman she had slandered wished. The following Sunday she would occupy the stool of repentance in the Cathedral and there ask the forgiveness of God and the assembled congregation. There was yet another indignity to be suffered by Janet before then. Released at last from the manacles and branks which held her to the Tolbooth wall, she was escorted to the banks of the Clyde where she was publicly 'dowked' before a laughing, cheering crowd.

'Dowking' prisoners in the Clyde was a tricky and troublesome business ... the two men employed to carry out the punishment often finished up just as wet as the prisoner, and the special payment of five pennies was considered small reward for such a messy and demeaning chore. In 1587 the Kirk Session – empowered to impose and carry out these punishments – devised the perfect answer to this problem. A pulley was erected from which the women could be lowered into the Clyde, while the dispensers of the law remained high and dry on the ramparts of the Old Glasgow Bridge!

THE MURDER OF ROBERT PARK

ROBERT PARK was elected town clerk of Glasgow on 7 February, 1694. It was an office he was to hold proudly, albeit briefly.

Not long after Robert Park began his work, a certain Major James Menzies, then commanding a regiment stationed in the city, had arrested a number of citizens on the charge of being deserters from the armed forces. The citizens denied these charges and complaints were made to the city magistrates regarding the over zealous major. The magistrates then requested the major to bring his prisoners before them for trial. This he refused to do.

A meeting was arranged between the magistrates and the major. The meeting took place in the town clerk's office and soon developed into a raging argument between the town clerk and the soldier, in the course of which Major Menzies struck the town clerk across the face with his cane. The incensed official threw himself at the soldier and had to be restrained by the others present. While Robert Park was being thus restrained by his friends, Major Menzies drew his sword and ran him through the heart.

The murdering major then took to his heels pursued by outraged citizens who finally cornered him in a city garden. In the ensuing struggle Major Menzies was shot dead. But the drama was not yet over. It was alleged that Menzies had offered to surrender and had instead been shot in cold blood. In consequence of this three of his pursuers were then charged with murder.

The town council determined that no more blood should be shed in the affair, sent three of its most able magistrates to defend the prisoners who were eventually discharged after a lengthy and sensational trial.

Robert Park's reign as town clerk of Glasgow lasted exactly eight months.

RAISING HELL AT THE TRON

IN 1793 a town council minute recorded that the Tron Kirk was 'totally burned by accidental fire'. The citizens of Glasgow knew better.

It was common knowledge that the fire had been started by the drunken members of the city's Hellfire Club determined to discover just exactly how much hellfire they could get away with. Piling benches and chairs upon the session-house fire, they had laughed and sung in the flickering light until, even in their drunken state, it became obvious that the flames were spreading along the wooden floor and onto the timber walls of the adjoining church.

Soon the session-house and church were ablaze, and the fire burned until both buildings were reduced to ashes, leaving the Tron steeple alone and forlorn in the grey misty dawn. Sobered by the enormity of their crime the members of the Hellfire Club fled the city swearing never to return.

One member of the Club did return to the city though – Hugh Adamson, who in times past had ridiculed the Bible story of the Resurrection by parading the city graveyards at midnight, blowing a trumpet and commanding the dead to rise and walk the streets of Glasgow. On the 5 June, 1805, Hugh Adamson was hanged at Glasgow Cross, not for arson or blasphemy, but for the capital crime of forgery.

The Tron Kirk session-house was later rebuilt and became the meeting place of Glasgow's first police force in 1800. Here, along with other members of that first force, Jaiky Burns had reported for duty and had been issued with his lamp, candle, greatcoat, and four foot stave with his number painted upon it. He had marched to his sentry-box at the foot of the Candleriggs, 'called the hours' at 11 o'clock, then midnight – and then had his sentrybox pushed over on top of him by a roaming band of drunken weavers.

Trapped inside like a corpse in a coffin, he lay in impotent rage until rescued and relieved at four am. He then had to sweep the streets for two hours.

The collecting of street manure was part and parcel of the policeman's lot, and the sale of dung was a major source of revenue to the infant police force. A Statement of Receipts of 1814 records that 'dung of the streets' realised £418.15.2.

Begun with a strength of 80 men the police gradually grew in numbers and by 1824 the Gorbals, Calton, and Anderston Police forces had been instituted. In unruly Calton the police were forced to patrol in pairs armed with cutlasses, and on one occasion it is recorded that one pair severed the arm of a bodysnatcher in the Clyde Street burial ground. The assessment tax imposed for the upkeep of the police was very unpopular, and the Gorbals Police suffered the indignity of being turfed out of their own station by an angry mob who burned their books and records then defied the ousted police to 'come and get us – if you dare!'

SOUVENIRS OF A MURDERER

AMONG the many murders committed in Old Glasgow, that carried out by James McKean deserves special mention, if only because of the unusual and macabre events which took place after his execution.

On 7 October, 1796, McKean invited Andrew Buchanan into his home in the High Street and then murdered him by drawing an open razor across his throat. The last thing McKean would have expected to see was his own wife rush into the street screaming that bloody murder was being done. But she did.

McKean, like the old-time villain he was, snarled – 'Woman, you have done for me now!' And she had. His trial and sentence to death created a great sensation, and many lurid and gory tales were told of McKean's early life, the worst being that he had murdered his own mother in order to inherit a small property she had owned. This story caused so much speculation in the city that the clergyman attending to McKean's last needs was prevailed upon to ask him if he had indeed committed this terrible crime.

'Can you keep a secret?' asked McKean, lowering his voice. 'I can,' promised the clergyman. 'Good,' whispered McKean. 'And so can I.'

After his execution in 1797, McKean's body was handed over to the University authorities for dissection and anatomical study. The anatomist was then approached by a group of city merchants with an unusual request – could they have the skin from the back of McKean?

The skin was duly handed over, tanned, cut into circles, then distributed as mementos of the notorious Glasgow murderer.

CHAPTER 7

Glasgow and the Clyde

A REPORT OF 1656 stated that the River Clyde was so shallow that 'no vessels of any burden could come nearer to Glasgow than 14 miles'. This explains why the city's shipping port at that time was to be found at Cunningham on the Ayrshire coast.

Despite the difficulty of bringing ships into the heart of town in 1662 it was decided 'for many guid reasons' that there should be 'ane little key builded at the Broomielaw'. The 'little key' was duly 'builded' at a cost of £166.13.4.

The city magistrates then decided that a harbour was needed closer to hand, and an attempt was made to purchase land at Dumbarton for this purpose. Dumbarton refused to sell and gave the excuse that 'the great influx of mariners would raise the price of provisions to the inhabitants'. The Glasgow magistrates replied to this by buying 13 acres of land on the south side of the river and creating Port Glasgow. The first graving dock in Scotland was constructed there.

With the passing of time, the conviction grew that the future prosperity of the city depended upon improvements to the river, and in 1740 it was resolved to 'go the length of £100 sterling to build a flat-bottomed boat to carry off the sand and the shingle from the banks of the river'. In this modest fashion was begun the great task of transforming the gentle Clyde into the ocean highway which was later to spawn the mightiest ships the world would ever see.

And in this modest fashion was also begun the unanswerable question – did Glasgow make the Clyde, or did the Clyde make Glasgow? But it wasn't just for its BIG ships that the Clyde was famous – the little ships had their place, too. Take, for example, the *Cluthas* ...

IT WAS ON a cold and raw April morning in 1884, before dawn had time to break over the river, that a little passenger steamer, *Clutha No 1*, left the landing stage at Victoria Bridge and began the 45 minute journey that would take it to another 11 landing stages along the river. At Springfield Lane or Stobcross, at Pointhouse or Partick, at Water Row or Linthouse, workers would embark or disembark, paying their penny fare and thanking God and the Clyde Trust for the introduction of 'The Penny Steamers'. This new passenger service was an immediate success and the fleet of four ships was promptly increased to 12. Soon they were carrying up to three and a half million passengers a year and showing their owners a tidy profit.

The Cluthas – Gaelic for Clyde – became a major feature of the river as they scurried their way between the large coastal steamers and cargo ships thronging the busy waterway, and it became as natural for a Glaswegian to hop aboard a Clutha as it was later to hop aboard a tram.

And it was the advent of the electric tram and the subway that was to sound the death knell of the Penny Steamer. On 30 November, 1903, *Clutha No 11* left Glasgow Bridge for the last time and sailed quietly into the pages of Glasgow's maritime history.

ANOTHER memorable day in the history of the river began much earlier. In November, 1784, the cold hand of winter took hold of the town and its inhabitants and held them in an iron grip of frost and ice such as the people had never known. From the sturdy mansions alongside the Cathedral to the ramshackle lodging-houses in the Briggait, people shivered and prayed for an early Spring.

In December the river began to freeze as fingers of ice stretched daily farther and farther from each bank until at last they met and held the waters in icy stillness. Children began to play upon the frozen waste that had once been the liquid, flowing heart of Glasgow. Their elders, shamed by youthful courage, began to join them, and soon it seemed as though half of Glasgow was enjoying the novelty of strolling upon the frozen river. Booths were opened along the river's edge as shopkeepers rushed to join their customers, while on the ice itself dram-shops with fire in them began to flourish. Great was the trade as fathers stopped amusing their sliding, skating children to recharge their flagging energies with foaming ale and heart-warming whiskies.

Nothing lasts forever, however, and on 4 March, 1785, after four long months of ice-bound captivity, the Clyde began to flow freely once more and a unique episode came to an end.

Three years earlier the river had provided sport of another sort. On 11 March, 1782, the citizens of Glasgow went to bed wondering just where all the rain was coming from. They certainly knew where it was going! For days it had been falling in a steady, unending downpour that had seen the broad and shallow Clyde – unfettered by jetties and other restraining influences – grow steadily broader and deeper.

They awoke on the morning of 12 March to find boats floating down the Saltmarket, Bridgegate, Jamaica Street and Stockwell Street. Before the water finally subsided, it had reached a remarkable 20 feet above normal, and Gorbals village was left standing like an island in an estuary.

Later, in 1795 another flood destroyed the newly erected stone bridge at the foot of the Saltmarket. The displaced water rushed across the Low Green with such force that the doors of the public wash-house were burst open and great quantities of clothing washed away in the flood. All along the banks of the river there was a great loss of grain and cattle, with 'flocks, herds, and harvests' floating through the city for hours. Even the Mutton Market in King Street was inundated – with the beneficial side-effect that all the rats drowned!

These floods were a seasonal hazard to the hardy citizens of the Briggait who had often been warned that their drunken and dissolute lifestyle would one day be punished by the raging waters of the Clyde.

Hawkie, character and wit that he was, also predicted the destruction of the Briggait by flooding, only in his version it would be whisky and not water that would reach to the highest windows in the street. Hundreds would be rescued in wooden tubs, said Hawkie, but many more would be drowned as they leaned over the side to sample the heady delights of their very own river of whisky!

CHAPTER 8

The Daphne Disaster

AT 11.20 AM on 3 July, 1883, Alexander Stephen's shipbuilding yard at Linthouse was the scene of intense activity as preparations for the launching of the 500-ton steamer Daphne neared completion.

With only minutes to go before launching time, there were still more than 200 workmen on board. Under normal conditions only essential staff would have been aboard at this time, but the yard would soon be closing for the Glasgow Fair holidays and so the rush was on to have her handed over to her owners, the Glasgow and Londonderry Steam Packet Company.

All over the Daphne, in the passageways and cabins, in the engine and boiler-rooms, above and below decks, men continued with their work as the dog-shores were knocked away and the ship began her smooth descent along the slipway towards the waiting waters of the Clyde.

Alfred Martin and William Vogwell were two of the men who helped to knock away the dog-shores. Just a few moments earlier they had been aboard the Daphne, working alongside their two companions and fellow Englishmen, John Lahive and Henry Clark.

All four had come from Devonport just six weeks previously and had been looking forward to sharing the thrill of their first launch. A foreman, however, had commandeered Martin and Vogwell to assist with the dogshores and so there they were, disgruntled and disappointed, watching the ship move away, envious of everyone on board.

James McLean, on the other hand, envied everyone on shore. He couldn't explain it to himself, and he would never have dreamed of trying to explain it to anyone else, but he had a premonition that something dreadful was about to happen. That was why he ensured that he was working on deck rather than down below. And that was why he had been carrying a large spar of wood all morning. No matter where he moved to his spar of wood was lifted and taken with him. No one noticed. People were much too busy doing their own work to be interested in what anyone else was doing. Everyone was occupied.

Except William Telfer. William Telfer had nothing to do and all day to do it in, he wasn't a member of any squad on board the Daphne, neither was he a shipyard worker. A 21-year-old Govan dentist who had come to see the launch, Telfer had decided that the best place to see it was from the deck of the Daphne. He had walked aboard the ship unchallenged and was strolling about the deck showing great interest in all that was going on. He had told his mother that he was going to see the launch and was more than excited about telling her that he had been a part of it!

The Daphne was moving fast along the slipway, picking up speed as she neared the dark and turgid waters of the river. And then she was in. All those aboard stopped work as she entered water for the first time and heeled to port – now she would return to an even keel, settle, and allow work to continue.

But the Daphne did not return to an even keel. After a feeble attempt to right herself she stopped, hung steady for a brief, breathless moment, then continued her heel to port as men were sent sprawling and sliding along the sloping deck and down into the murky waters of the Clyde. Those who had somehow managed to hold on to the port rail found themselves bombarded by the plates and deck planks that had been lifted so that the boilers could be later dropped into place.

In a moment the river was full of drowning, bleeding men.

Water poured unrestrainedly into the hold and boiler room while horrified onlookers watched in shocked disbelief as the unthinkable happened – and the Daphne sank and disappeared beneath the water she had entered just a moment before.

A number of men had clambered over the starboard rail and were now standing on the side of the ship, the waters of the Clyde lapping around their waists. The scene, frozen forever into the minds of all who were present, then exploded into one of frantic action as boats and tugs raced forward in a desperate rescue operation.

James McLean, whose spar of wood had been wrenched from his

hands when the Daphne heeled over, was struggling desperately to stay afloat, his strength draining away, his worst fears about to be realised, when a line thrown from the tug Hotspur fell across his face. He was then hauled aboard, one of the last to be plucked alive from the suddenly deadly Clyde.

News of the tragedy spread like wildfire through the streets of Govan, and soon there was a stream of wives and mothers pouring into the yard seeking news of husbands and sons, fathers and brothers.

The search for bodies began, and at 1.15pm the first was brought ashore. By the end of the day the figure had reached 41. A temporary morgue was set up in one of the spar-houses and bodies were laid out for inspection and identification. They included a 14-year-old rivet boy, a 21-year-old dentist, a 25-year-old engineer due to be married the following day, and two Englishmen recently arrived from Devonport.

On Wednesday, 4 July, a telegram arrived from Queen Victoria, expressing her grief at the disaster and hoping that reports of loss of life were exaggerated. They were not. She was later to contribute £100 towards a relief fund for dependants.

In the days that followed various attempts were made to refloat the Daphne without success. Bodies began to float to the surface of the river, and by Sunday the total dead amounted to 75. Funeral processions became a familiar and seemingly endless sight in the streets of Govan and Partick.

By 14 July, Fair Saturday, the Daphne had been partly raised, with the bridge-house and upper deck visible at low tide. Holiday-makers going 'doon the watter' had a perfect view of the salvage operations. Not until 21 July, however, was the Daphne finally floated and persuaded to give up all her dead. In cabins and passageways, behind doors and stairways, beneath the four foot of mud and silt that had gathered in the hold of the sunken ship, body after body was found. In total, 124 men were killed.

It was a disaster without parallel in the history of the Clyde. But how did it happen? What caused the Daphne to heel to such an extent that she was unable to right herself? At the official inquiry headed by Sir Edward Reed, the yard manager, Robert McMaster, was in no doubt as to the cause: 'My opinion,' he said, 'is that the ship was entirely tripped by the flood tide coming up the river, and the current coming down.' Others believed that the drag chains used to slow the ship when she entered the water had been at fault. Sir Edward, however, rejected these as causes and found that 'the cause of the accident was not to be found outside of the Daphne herself, and all of the evidence goes to show that the Daphne was well and effectually launched.' The inquiry was then led to the question of the initial stability of the Daphne, and it was here that Sir Edward was to lay the blame for the tragedy.

Aggravated by the sudden movement of 28 tons of loose materials, added to the shifting weight of 195 workmen when the Daphne first heeled to port, this lack of initial stability was, he found, the sole cause of the disaster.

Exonerating the builders and owners on the grounds that the estimation of a ship's stability on strictly scientific lines was at that time practised by no one in the shipbuilding trade, Sir Edward recommended that when ships were ordered in the future more consideration should be given to this problem.

The whole question of stability was investigated by naval architects and builders, and systems of calculation were eventually formulated to cover the life of a ship from launch to old age.

The lives lost by the capsizing of the Daphne were not, after all, to have been lost in vain.

CHAPTER 9

Glasgow's Bailies

PASSING A CITY BAILIE in the street the average Glaswegian would no more think of doffing his cap to him than to any other passer-by. But this wasn't always so!

In times gone by, failure to show proper respect to the city's velvet-coated bailies and magistrates would lead to the offender being marched to Glasgow Cross, bare headed and bare footed, to ask pardon for his crimes.

And woe betide anyone foolish enough to voice disapproval or disagreement regarding the decisions reached by these stout guardians of law and order. A muttered complaint by one Patrick Adam on 12 February, 1642, was enough to have him incarcerated in the Tolbooth prison for eight days.

When one realises that his cell was dark and damp, that he was without bed or blanket, that his meagre supply of food consisted of gruel and cold water, and that any further complaints on his part would have led to the jailer laying about his head with a large and heavy stick, then the enormity of Patrick's punishment becomes somewhat clearer.

Small wonder the honest citizens of Glasgow showed proper respect and deference before their bailies – what they said behind their backs was something else altogether.

And being such proud and solemn fellows it was perhaps inevitable that our civic forefathers should become a prime target of the local jokesters and storytellers. One bailie, administering justice in the town hall, was said to have been told of a pet squirrel that had escaped from the person in whose care it had been left. Informed that the squirrel had made its departure via an open window the bailie enquired as to why its wings had not been clipped.

'The squirrel is a quadruped, your honour,' explained the somewhat embarrassed defendant.

'Quadruped or no', snapped the bailie, 'if ye had clippit the brute's wings it couldnae hae flown awa!'

His fellow bailies were said to have nodded vigorous approval at the handing down of this pearl of wisdom.

And the wife of one newly-elected bailie, it was said, complained to a friend that her husband was so proud of being on the town council that he had refused to take his soup 'Jist because the dish-cloot had been biled in it.'

The bailie best known to our ancient ancestors was a gentleman whose real name is lost in antiquity and who is now known only by the nickname he was given after he found a group of workmen hanging a portrait of King Charles the Second in the Town Hall.

The sight of the workmen hanging the portrait of the king – with their heads covered – was too much for the officious bailie. 'Uncover your heads,' he roared. 'You are in the presence of Royalty.'

Bidding the fearful workers to fall to their knees (or hunkers) before the offended portrait he led them in a public apology to the unsmiling and unhearing king. He was ever afterwards known as Bailie Hunkers.

Out on official business one day the proud bailie was said to have found his path blocked by the lumbering antics of a travelling Italian and his performing bear. Impatient to pass, Bailie Hunkers drew his civic sword and prodded the large and shaggy rump before him.

The bear, thinking perhaps that he had found another dancing partner, swept the startled Hunkers into his arms and continued the dance which ended only when bear and bailie fell headlong into an open pit of the kind then used to contain human waste.

For this horrendous crime the bear was arrested and sentenced to be shot as a warning to all bears not to offend the dignity of Glasgow's bailies. Flanked by a party of town-officers the bear was led, bound, along the Gallowgate to the Butts, an area of open land later to become the site of the Cavalry Barracks. Here, before a large crowd, and after the firing of a great many shots, the dancing bear was duly executed.

The bear's owner was treated less harshly. After his capture in the Cathkin Braes the Italian, Antonio Dallon, was forced to spend an hour in the stocks at Glasgow Cross with the skin of his erstwhile companion draped around his shoulders. Seeing the familiar shaggy coat the poor Italian burst into tears of inconsolable sorrow and the Glasgow mob were so touched that not a single missile was thrown at the grieving prisoner.

CHAPTER 10

A Bishop's Mighty Dream

ON A WARM and sunny summer's day in the year 1195, Jocelyn, Bishop of Glasgow, stood and watched as workmen laboured over the building of his beloved cathedral. The sound of hammer on chisel was music to his ears, and he smiled encouragement to any mason or carpenter whose eye met his.

The boundless energy that drove Jocelyn ever forward into new enterprises and new beginnings urged him to take hammer in hand and speed the work which proceeded so slowly and ponderously. Only the dignity of office stopped him from putting thought into action.

And besides, he told himself, he was getting a little too old for such strenuous labour. Better to leave it to these young and healthy Glaswegians whose pride and craftsmanship were better suited to the task of raising a house to God than his own eager but unskilled hands.

Instead, he moved to the edge of the hill and looked down with pleasure and affection upon the little town whose destiny and welfare had occupied the past 20 years of his life.

His bright and kindly eyes took in a vista of green forest and silver stream, thatched roofs and rambling tracks, grazing cattle and industrious farmers. How often he had stood here and gazed down upon this scene, and had often followed the path down to the market cross to see for himself the slow and gradual expansion of the burgh whose existence he had been so instrumental in bringing into being.

IN 1175, the very year of his consecration, he had wrested from William the Lion, King of Scotland, a charter proclaiming Glasgow a burgh of barony, freeing the town from the rapacious clutches of Rutherglen and Dumbarton, and opening the way for merchants and craftsmen to prosper under the kindly dictatorship of their own bishop. An impish smile crossed his face as he remembered the rage and indignant frustration of his larger and more important neighbours.

For too long the little wealth that Glasgow possessed had been drained away to fill the pockets and increase the prosperity of Rutherglen. However, the sphere of its influence had been curtailed and would soon be restricted to the Cross of Sheddinstoun (Shettleston). The cries of pain and outrage at such a loss of revenue would, he was sure, be heard all the way to the Cross of Glasgow.

The tightrope of diplomacy between Church and King was one that Jocelyn walked with grace and dexterity – and profit. He had repaid the favour of the King's charter by going to Rome and securing the removal of the excommunication imposed upon William at the insistence of Henry of England and the Archbishop of York – then obtained from the grateful King yet another charter allowing Glasgow the all-important right to hold an annual Fair!

Profit had been his motive behind the commissioning and sale of a book on the *Life and Miracles of Saint Kentigern*. The money was wanted, not to increase the personal wealth of the bishop, but to purchase materials and to pay for the labour required in the building of the new cathedral.

In 1136 a great fire had destroyed the cathedral, and Jocelyn planned to build another to take its place. It would be his final gift to the people of the town, a church of high magnificence which would stand above this holy ground, visible to the farmer toiling in the field, the weaver at his loom, and the fisherman drawing his net heavy with salmon. How many churches had been raised on this hallowed ground, he wondered ... how many rude and humble dwellings dedicated to the glory of God and the civilising of Man?

Here Ninian had planted his Cross, and here Mungo had built his church, a church dimmed by the obscurity of five dark and mysterious centuries. Would his church be lost to future generations? Would the toil and the sweat of such endeavour vanish into the mist of time and become a half-remembered legend?

Or would it stand forever, proclaiming to one and all the message so joyfully spread by past and future churchmen – that Glasgow and its Cathedral would flourish, by the preaching of the Word, and the labour of its people. Jocelyn chose to believe that it would.

CHAPTER 11

The Bishop's Palace

THE BISHOP'S PALACE, also known as the Castle of Glasgow, existed in various forms for almost 500 years. Standing on the ground now occupied by the Royal Infirmary and the St Mungo Museum of Religious Life and Art in Castle Street, it had begun its life as a fortified home for Glasgow's Roman Catholic bishops.

Succeeding bishops added their own contributions to the building of the Palace, and in the 15th century the final touches were added to what had become a magnificent structure. Within the spacious grounds were stables, gardens, orchards, and a palace fitting the style and the taste of Bishop Cameron, the most princely of all the prelates ever to occupy the See of Glasgow.

Having set his own house in order, the bishop then ordered his prebendaries to build their parsonages within the immediate area. The building of these fine houses did much to increase the trade, size, and appearance of Glasgow. Being the home of the city's bishops, one might have expected the palace to have been a model of spiritual solemnity and Christian compassion and it very often was. It was also, however, the scene of bloody conflict and betrayal.

In 1300 it was here that the English troops of Edward I were garrisoned when William Wallace and his army charged up the High Street to defeat them in the Battle o' the Brae ... and in 1544 the Regent Arran promised clemency to the soldiers of the Earl of Lennox who had defied his fierce onslaught for ten long days. The embattled garrison, tired, hungry, aware of the impossibility of reinforcements, accepted the offer with grateful promptitude ... and with equal promptitude were put to death.

Only once did the palace fall to the force of arms, when in 1517 John

Muir of Caldwell captured and ransacked the home of Glasgow's bishop. The enraged prelate went to law and demanded the return not only of his jewels, silks, and precious stones, but also 15 swine, 6 dozen salmon, six barrels of gunpowder – and 28 feather beds!

By 1560 the Reformation had taken such a hold on the minds of men that the reigning prelate, Archbishop Beaton, was forced to run for France, taking with him the charters, documents, gold and silver pertaining to the See and University of Glasgow. It is believed that these ancient treasures were stored in the Scots College in Paris and were eventually destroyed by rampaging mobs during the carnage of the French Revolution.

After the Reformation in Scotland, the Bishop's Palace fell into steady decline, but even when finally demolished with only the courtyard remaining, the scenes of violence and bloodshed continued with the setting up of the public gallows on which 12 criminals were eventually to meet their end.

In 1754 the ruins of the once mighty palace were carted away to be used in the building of the Saracen's Head Inn and the Castle of Glasgow ceased to exist.

CHAPTER 12

Witchcraft

WHEN THE Scottish Parliament passed its first statute against witchcraft in 1563 a reign of terror was begun that was to last for almost 200 years. The injunction of the Old Testament that 'thou shalt not suffer a witch to live' was followed with a vengeance!

At one sitting of Parliament in Edinburgh 600 people were indicted for witchcraft, while in Glasgow there was a 'great business for the trial of witches'. Business was so great in 1697 that the Glasgow jailer was given a special payment of £68.8.0 Scots 'for the maintenance of the witches and warlocks here in the Tolbooth'.

Warlocks (male witches) were far outnumbered by their female counterparts. King James VI wrote a book on the subject and explained the reason for this – the Devil had always been on homelier terms with the women! And it was the women who suffered most at the hands of the Witchfinder, the state official whose task it was to test the accused witch. His powers were terrifying. It was said that those who had sold their soul to the Devil had been touched by Satan during their initiation ceremony and that the spot so touched was forever afterwards devoid of feeling and blood. All the Witchfinder had to do was find that spot.

Stripping the accused naked, he would prick over her entire body with a large needle called a 'brod' until he found a spot from which no blood could be extracted. This was immediately declared to be the 'witch-mark', and the fate of the accused was sealed. If there was difficulty in locating the dreaded mark – and there often was – then the Witchfinder had a simple solution. His needle, set in a secret spring, would be retracted, the accused would not be pricked, did not bleed, and was therefore declared a witch!

Under torture the 'witch' would then admit to the most impossible of crimes. Among the less horrific of tortures would be the force feeding of salted food and the denial of drinking water. At the other end of the torture list was the iron boot which crushed flesh and bone so much that 'blood and marrow spouted forth in great abundance'. It was believed that by torturing the 'witch' the Devil himself was also being punished and so the inflicting of pain on witches and warlocks had the double advantage of being encouraged by the State and blessed by the Church.

One well-known case of witchcraft concerned Sir George Maxwell of Pollok who, while inspecting his soap and candle works in the Candleriggs of Glasgow, was suddenly seized with a great pain that racked his shoulder and side. Rushed to his home in Pollok House he lay in bed flushed with a violent heat. His doctors were at a loss to explain his illness or to offer a cure.

Jenny Douglas, a deaf and mute vagrant, appeared at the door. She led the laird's family to a nearby cottage which was the home of John Mathie, recently imprisoned for stealing fruit belonging to the laird. Behind the chimney of the cottage the family found a wax figure with pins pushed through its side and shoulder. The pins were removed and the sick laird immediately began to mend.

A month later Sir George was ill once again, hovering on the brink of death. Once more the cottage was searched and another pin-stuck figure was found.

John Mathie, his sister, and three other women were arrested and charged with witchcraft. All denied the charge until witch-marks were declared to have been found on both Mathie and his sister who then confessed their alliance with the Devil 'a man dressed in black, with hoggars over his bare feet, which were cloven.' The warlock and four witches were strangled before being burned at the stake in Paisley on 20 February, 1677.

CHAPTER 13

The Resurrectionists

THE THOUGHT of digging up bodies in a darkened cemetery is enough to disgust and horrify the majority of Glasgow's citizens today, but this wasn't always the case!

In the early part of the 19th century medical schools in Glasgow and Edinburgh were packed with students thirsting for knowledge of the human body, and the only way to gain that knowledge was by the dissection and examination of a human corpse. The number of corpses legally available was never enough, and bodysnatching became a brisk, and at times profitable, business.

In 1812 a sloop from Ireland discharged a cargo of linen rags, that then lay unclaimed in a Broomielaw shed for several days. The unusual smell coming from the sacks aroused such comment that they were eventually opened – to reveal the bodies of men, women, and children, bound for the dissecting tables of Glasgow and Edinburgh Colleges. The scandal caused by this discovery ended the wholesale import of bodies into Scotland, and the anatomists were reduced to the occasional unclaimed corpse from the city hospitals. Until 1818 the occasional body from the city hangman was available, but this source was stopped after the sensational, celebrated, (and highly exaggerated) 'coming to life' of hanged murderer Mathew Clydesdale during experiments being conducted by the famous Dr James Jeffray. (See p89.)

The students of anatomy increasingly turned to grave-robbing, and were called 'The Resurrectionists' (the body-snatchers). By 1823 a state of affairs had been reached where armed guards had to be placed in the city graveyards in an effort to foil the midnight diggers. Bereaved families were forced to protect graves by placing an iron gate (mort-safe) over them, and by the even more drastic measure of installing trip-guns.

Revolting and gruesome as the sorry business was, being Glasgow it was not without its moments of black humour.

A student is said to have been killed by a trip-gun in Blackfriars churchyard in the High Street and his dead body returned to his lodgings by two of his fellow resurrectionists who tied his legs to their own and carried him between them through the city streets, singing loudly and staggering drunkenly. This behaviour raised little interest in a district well used to the high spirits and drinking habits of the college inmates!

On another occasion two watchmen guarding the grave of a recently-buried townsman arrived at the churchyard to discover their client's body packed snugly away in a sack, ready to be carried off by students who were at that moment making sure that the coast was clear before venturing into the streets with their 'bundle'. One of the watchmen promptly changed places with the corpse and was duly lifted onto the shoulder of a brawny student who proceeded to head towards the area of the college. Unsure of his way through the darkened streets the perspiring student asked his companion which way they should go, at which the 'corpse' in the sack reached out, grabbed him by the hair, and cried in a deathly voice: 'Doon the Rottenrow, ye scoundrel!'

It's doubtful if this particular student ever went body-snatching again.

Finding it increasingly difficult to obtain bodies in Glasgow, students were forced to go further afield for their specimens, and consequently faced greater risk of detection when they transported bodies back to the city.

One pair of students solved this problem by dressing their corpse in a suit of fine clothes and placing him between them on the seat of their gig as they drove from the Mearns to Glasgow. Stopping at the Gorbals toll-bar to pay their dues they explained to the toll-keeper that their companion was feeling 'a wee bittie under the weather'.

Looking closely at the corpse, the kindly but obviously short-sighted toll-keeper nodded in sympathy and said 'Poor auld bodie, he looks unco ill in the face. Drive cannily, lads, drive cannily.'

IN DECEMBER, 1813, however, there was very little comedy to be found in the city streets. The Cathedral Churchyard and the Ramshorn

Churchyard in Ingram Street had both been desecrated and a newly interred body stolen from each. As news of the outrage spread through the city furious mobs converged upon the university medical school, throwing stones at the building and threatening the lives of all inside.

Police, armed with a magistrate's search warrant, made a lightning raid upon the college, and, despite denials and protestations of innocence, within moments had discovered, beneath floorboards, various parts of a human body. These remains were quickly identified as those of Mrs McAllister, the woman whose body had been stolen from the Ramshorn Churchyard. On 6 June, 1814, Dr G S Pattison and three others stood trial charged with 'ruthlessly and feloniously' violating the grave of Mrs McAllister, stealing her body, and taking it to their dissecting rooms 'where it was found and identified'.

During the course of the sensational trial, however, it was proved that, whoever the portions of the body belonged to, they had not belonged to Mrs McAllister, and so Dr Pattison and his friends were duly acquitted.

The grisly and scandalous traffic in bodies continued until matters were brought to a head with the trial in Edinburgh of Burke and Hare, the most notorious of all the body-snatchers.

There was a curious little postscript to this trial, when the Glasgow Chronicle of 10 February, 1829, reported an attack upon Hare's wife by a Glasgow mob. The woman had been recognised in the Broomielaw as she tried vainly to find a ship to take her back to Ireland. Taken to the Calton police station for her own safety she declared that she had been four nights in Glasgow 'with her infant and bit duds' and wished nothing more than to return to her native land. On 12 February her wish was granted and she was put aboard the steamer Fingal bound for Belfast.

Shortly after the trial of Burke and Hare the Anatomy Act was passed, and arrangements were made by law for the supply of bodies for anatomical studies. Years later, when the work of the Resurrectionists could be discussed calmly and rationally, Dr Richard Millar, Professor of Medicine at Glasgow University, felt himself able to declare that 'These experiments, at the Glasgow School of Anatomy, lighted up the torch of science, and saved the lives of many invaluable human beings.'

CHAPTER 14

Some Famous 'Old Glasgow' Men

KIRKMAN FINLAY

WHEN KIRKMAN FINLAY was elected Member of Parliament for Glasgow and the Clyde Burghs in 1812 medals were struck in his honour and joyous crowds drew his open coach all the way from Glasgow Cross to his mansion in Queen Street. Later, when he voted for Prosperity Robinson's Corn Bill, the same crowds rushed all the way to his mansion once more – to stone it!

It was a rebuke he took in his capable stride. One of the shrewdest of Glasgow's merchantmen, Kirkman Finlay had tackled and beaten bigger game than the fickle Glasgow mob. Napoleon, for example.

When Bonaparte had issued the Berlin Decree of 1806 declaring the British Isles to be in a state of blockade, Finlay quickly became one of Britain's most successful blockade-runners, establishing depots at strategic points on the Continent and organising a great trade in British goods across the forbidden frontiers of Europe. The risks were high ... but so too were the rewards.

Finlay also tackled the mighty East India Company. For two centuries the Company held the monopoly of all trade east of the Cape of Good Hope, and Finlay agitated strongly for an opening up of this trade.

No sooner was this door opened than he had freighted the Earl of Buckinghamshire and sent it post-haste to Bombay, the first ship to sail direct from the Clyde to an Eastern port. He was the first to send a Glasgow ship to Calcutta, and later sent his own ship, the Kirkman Finlay direct from the Clyde to China.

Few men did more to establish the international reputation of Glasgow's hard-headed and hard-hitting merchant adventurers.

JAMES MCRAE

IN 1692 JAMES MCRAE, son of a poor washerwoman of Ayr, ran away to sea. Forty years later he returned a man of rank and the possessor of an immense fortune.

McRae's early life at sea was shrouded in mystery, but it was rumoured that his apprenticeship was served under the black flag of piracy. What is known about him is that he later joined the East India Company and that his brilliant career there led to his appointment as Governor of Madras.

Shortly after his return to his native land McRae was made a burgess of Glasgow, and in appreciation of this honour he presented the city with the gift of a statue. For more than a century and a half it stood in the Trongate, adored by many, abused by not a few.

The statue was the equestrian statue of King William of Orange. Towards the end of the 19th century the Trongate was widened to accommodate the increasing traffic of the city, and 'King Billy', dressed for some unknown reason in the garb of a Roman Emperor was forced to move. He and his noble steed were put out to pasture in the more rural surroundings of Cathedral Square. The horse's tail, set in a ball and socket joint, is reputed to sway lazily when high winds shake the trees and scatter leaves across the ancient square.

JAMES MONTEITH

WHEN THE PLUNDERING REIVERS of Rob Roy McGregor drove Henry Monteith from his lands in Aberfoyle they could have had no idea of the chain of events they had set in motion.

Monteith settled in the village of Anderston and took up life as a market gardener, but had the good sense to apprentice his son James into the weaving trade. Hard work, business acumen, and the courage to take calculated risks raised the humble weaver to a pre-eminent position as a large-scale manufacturer of muslin and cambric, and Glasgow's largest importer of foreign yarn. Creating employment for many hundreds of Glaswegians, James became a leading force in the development of the great weaving and spinning industry of the city. By 1787 the demand for cotton yarn was so great that spinning mills were being built alongside every fast flowing river within the Glasgow area, and the city's population began to expand at an extraordinary rate.

Small wonder, then, that James Monteith came to be spoken of as the father of the Glasgow cotton industry, and the driving force behind the city's second great era of prosperity – tobacco, of course, being the first. From his home in Bishop Street Monteith sent forth six sons each of whom were to have great effect upon the commercial and social life of Glasgow. But it was his third son, Henry, born in 1764, who was to become the most illustrious of this great clan. Appointed Lord Provost in the years 1815-16 and 1819-20, Henry went on to represent his native city as Member of Parliament. The elegant Monteith Row was named after him.

WALTER STIRLING

WALTER STIRLING, a Glasgow merchant, entered the home of James Wardrop in high good humour. He had been invited, most unexpectedly, to join a supper party there, and, being well aware of Wardrop's reputation as a generous and entertaining host, had gladly accepted. Wardrop also had a reputation as a joker and stager of elaborate and costly games. Stirling wondered what amusing and diverting ploy had he arranged for this evening? He entered the elegant and brightly lit room and gazed around the assembled guests. Their cheery and smiling faces were unknown to him, but as he looked towards them he realised that Wardrop had played his joke for the evening and that he, Walter Stirling, was the butt of it. All the guests were, like Stirling himself, hunchbacks. While the others were obviously enjoying the joke it was not something that Walter Stirling found amusing. This sentiment he conveyed most forcefully to Wardrop and his fellow guests before storming out of the house never to return.

But if Stirling's sense of humour sometimes failed him then his sense of duty to his fellow citizens never did. Even at his death his regard for his fellow men was shown by his establishment of a fund by which the city's first public library was brought into being.

Stirling's Library was established in 1791 and has had many homes – the most famous being of course the old Royal Exchange building in Queen Street. This fine building is now the Gallery of Modern Art and houses among other treasures The Library at Goma. Mr Stirling would surely have approved.

GEORGE GIBSON

IN 1780 GEORGE GIBSON was appointed bellman of Glasgow, was immediately named Bell Geordie, and in the words of a famous city chamberlain 'No one ever paced the Trongate who was better known or longer remembered.'

Geordie had won his appointment against fierce competition, for the post of bellman paid £10 per year, plus a fee for every item called around the town. A boatload of 'fine fresh herring, selling at three a penny' was worth a shilling to him, so also were the goods sold by the Gallowgate grocer 'who has taken an oath not to adulterate his tea!'

Resplendent in his cocked hat, scarlet coat, blue breeches and silver buckled shoes, Geordie would stroll the city streets ringing his mighty bell and proclaiming the wares and services of tailors, wigmakers, hoteliers and dancing masters.

Undertakers would employ him to advertise their latest fashions for 'dressing the dead', an important affair in those early days. The material used for 'last dresses' was specified by several Acts of Parliament, sometimes woollen, sometimes linen, depending upon which industry was most in need of help. Perhaps the call that Bell Geordie enjoyed most was the one which entreated thirsty Glaswegians to sample the delights of brandy and rum at 12 shillings a gallon!

ROBERT DREGHORN

IN THE EARLY 19TH CENTURY Robert Dreghorn was said to be the ugliest man in Glasgow and was known the city over as 'Bob Dragon'. Smallpox had deprived him of an eye and collapsed his nose flat upon his pock-marked face. His name was used by distracted mothers to frighten their troublesome children, and the cry of 'Bob Dragon!' was enough to scatter even the noisiest group of midnight revellers. He was, however, one of the wealthiest men in town.

From his stately mansion at the corner of Great Clyde Street and Rope Work Lane he would stroll daily, dressed in the height of fashion and following in the footsteps of every pretty maiden who passed his way. He became one of the sights of the city as he weaved a joyful and erratic course in pursuit of every rustling petticoat that happened to pass. He was, they said, the most observed of all observers. Despite his notorious and pitiable interest in the ladies, he died by his own hand, a rich and lonely bachelor.

Long after his death the name of Bob Dragon lingered on, with his house reputed to be haunted, and reports of his sad and ugly ghost seen wandering the midnight streets in search of a winsome smile and a well-turned ankle.

DAVID DALE

WHEN DAVID DALE left the Established church to join the Congregational Church he was, incredibly, stoned in the streets. Incredibly, because in the 18th century few men did more for Glasgow than the country boy from Stewarton, Ayrshire.

Arriving in Glasgow via Paisley and a weaving apprenticeship, he set up in business as a linen importer, prospering while endeavouring always to make business yield something more than mere profit. In 1784 he financed the building of cotton mills at New Lanark, employing an army of masons to build four mills and housing for over a thousand workers. His renown as a good and honest employer was enhanced when his son-in-law, Robert Owen, took over the mills and proceeded to build shops where workers could buy cheap food, and schools where their children could receive an education.

Dale opened more mills, in Dornoch and Oban, for the express purpose of providing work for hungry Highlanders, and when the price of meal rose beyond the reach of ordinary Glaswegians he imported great quantities of grain which was sold cheaply to the poor of the city.

He was a co-founder of the city's Chamber of Commerce and twice its chairman; a founder of the Humane Society and twice its president; a member of the Town Council and twice a magistrate!

His abandonment of the established church eventually came to be accepted by the people of his adopted city, and his death in 1806 was mourned by all sections of the public.

Probably the greatest philanthropist the city had known, he was at a loss to explain his amazing ability to amass wealth. 'I gave my money to God in handfuls,' he said. 'He gave it back to me in shovelfuls.'

CHAPTER 15

Unrelated People and Events

LICENSED TO BEG

THE BEGGAR LAY in his roughly-made cot, his twisted and crippled legs in full view of the family whose door he was carefully and deliberately placed beside. After a brief consultation with her husband the woman of the house poured a ladleful of oatmeal into the bag lying beside the poor creature. Her husband and son then carried the cot to the door of their nearest neighbour, and returned home relieved at having rid themselves of the unwholesome and wretched vagrant.

For almost an hour the beggar lay groaning in pain, his cries rising higher and higher in an effort to draw out the stubborn and hard-hearted family at whose door he now found himself. When it finally became obvious that his pathetic cries were falling on deaf ears the crippled beggar rose to his feet, lifted his cot, then marched away to find another, more generous, family whose door he could lie before.

This was one of the many tricks used by the 50,000 beggars that the General Assembly estimated were living in Scotland in the 17th century. Glasgow had so many beggars that badges bearing the town's coat-of-arms were issued to all beggars born within the city. Those without badges were then taken to the outskirts of town and ordered not to return.

Those who did return were branded across the cheek by a red hot iron.

SERMON THAT BUILT AN INN

IN 1727 a number of Highland gentlemen met in Glasgow to discuss the plight of their less fortunate kinsmen living in the city. Great concern was expressed for the jobless Highlanders and their children, who, 'though found to be of good genius were yet lost for want of education'.

The Glasgow Highland Society was formed to provide that education and for 30 years they struggled with few resources to clothe, train, and pay apprenticeship fees for almost 100 boys. More funds were needed, and when the famous preacher, George Whitefield, paid a visit to Glasgow in 1757 he was asked to give a sermon at which a collection could be made. The sermon was preached in the graveyard of Glasgow Cathedral and the collection afterwards was the largest made in the city up until that time.

With the accumulated funds now at their disposal the society purchased a piece of ground in Argyle Street and erected what was to become one of the city's most famous hotels – The Black Bull Inn.

With their annual income now greatly increased, the society could provide for a greater number of boys, and in 1788 they began their own schools. Later they were to begin day schools for girls. While the material needs of the children were the society's main concern, their spiritual needs were not forgotten. No boy was allowed to take up a trade unless he was first able to read the Bible, and all boys were constrained to attend Divine worship as it was said that nothing was more ruinous to youth than idle strolling upon a Sunday.

SHEDDING LIGHT
ON THE CANDLERIGGS

WHAT DOES the name of your street mean to you? Is it simply an address – or something more personal? The streets of Glasgow derive their names from many sources – distinguished persons, local worthies, historical events. If you live in Victoria Road then you probably know that it was named after Queen Victoria, and if Argyle Street is where you hang your hat then you may have guessed that it was named after the Duke of Argyll, although the spelling is different.

But how many Glaswegians know that Bath Street got its name from the city's first public baths that stood there, or that the Candleriggs once housed a candle works? How many Gorbalonians know that Hospital Street marks the site of Saint Ninian's Leper Hospital, where in the 14th century Glasgow would banish all citizens suffering from that dreaded disease?

Royalty are well represented in the city streets and include King George 3rd (George Square), Mary Queen of Scots (Queen Mary Avenue), and Queen Alexandra (Alexandra Parade). The lesser nobility can claim, among others, Cumberland Street (Duke of Cumberland), Eglinton Street (Duke of Eglinton), and Kent Street (Duke of Kent). Ordinary people could be immortalised on the city streets if they were elected Lord Provost. Provosts Ingram, Cochrane, Dunlop, Bain and Collins, were some of the city's 'first citizens' to be honoured in this way.

John Aird, five times Lord Provost, not only had a thoroughfare named after him (Aird's Lane) but also had the singular distinction of having a Street named in honour of his flock of geese (The Goosedubs, once one of the most fashionable streets in town).

If you were a successful businessman then you had every chance of being commemorated by a city street – Messrs Glassford, Orr, Millar, Buchanan, Balmano, Hutcheson, Dale and Dixon (of Dixon's Blazes) were among those who found lasting fame in his fashion.

If you were especially favoured and rich enough to buy your own land, you could have a whole district named after you. James Laurie bought himself a parcel of land on the south side of the river, laid out some streets, and called the area Laurieston. Mr Laurie had a liking for English place names, and so the streets in his own little kingdom were given names like Oxford, Norfolk, and Bedford. These 'foreign' names were accepted without too much fuss being made, but 'Bloomsbury' stuck in the Glasgow throat and was soon changed to the more acceptable 'Bridge Street'.

James Anderson of Stobcross is believed to have created two districts within the city. The village of Anderston he named after himself, and Finnieston he named after his tutor, the Reverend John Finnie.

Finnieston's other title, 'The World's End' came about when some destitute handloom weavers, depressed and disillusioned, swore they would go to the end of the world rather than live in such a wretched country. They packed their few belongings, marched out of town – and turned up later at the Little Loan in Finnieston!

In the years since the end of World War Two, the older citizens have seen Glasgow being dismantled before their very eyes, with streets and districts disappearing in clouds of dust and cascades of tired rubble.

Happily, many of the old street names have been retained. Happily, because they're not just labels to distinguish one street from another, but links in a chain that holds us, affectionately, to what seemed to be the sweet days of both our own, and the city's, youth.

DISASTER IN PANAMA

WILLIAM PATERSON, the Scotsman who founded the Bank of England then left because he felt its scope was too limited, conceived and engineered the Darien Expedition.

It was a breathtaking idea – a colony of Scottish traders operating from the Isthmus of Darien in Panama – the perfect trading post between Europe and the two Americas. The potential for profit seemed staggering and Paterson received subscriptions amounting to £400,000 – half the circulating capital of Scotland!

By Act of the Scottish Parliament in 1695, The Company of Scotland was formed to pursue and exploit the Darien dream, and in 1698 five ships sailed from Leith for Panama with 1200 Scots aboard. Further expeditions left from the Clyde, laden with goods stored in Glasgow warehouses, and bringing the total of colonists to 2700.

English trading companies, alarmed and afraid at this threat to markets they themselves desired, persuaded their Government to forbid the merchants of Jamaica, Barbados and New York the right to supply the Scottish colonists with the provisions needed to survive. Famine, followed by disease and despair, wreaked havoc with the struggling settlers. Spanish force of arms completed the task, and of the 2700 Scots who landed at Darien less than 300 are estimated to have returned to their homeland.

Collapse of the scheme almost caused national bankruptcy and many years were to pass before Scotland recovered from the dream that all too soon became a nightmare.

DUMBARTON CASTLE

WHEN THE EARL OF LENNOX led an army of English troops into Scotland his orders from Elizabeth of England were quite clear – spread fire and sword throughout the land of her enemy, Mary, Queen of Scots.

Lennox set to his task with a will. Towns were captured, homes destroyed, enemies vanquished. It seemed nothing could stand in his way.

Nothing, that is, except Dumbarton Castle.

The ancient 'Fortress of the Britons' had been under siege for many months and gave no sign of ever falling – until its commander, Lord Fleming, ordered the wife of a soldier to be flogged for stealing. The soldier, shamed and enraged at the punishment meted out to his wife, deserted the castle and offered his services to Lennox. He would lead his troops, he told the Earl, on an assault of the castle by the north-east wall, the highest and least likely to be well guarded.

Lennox placed the enterprise in the hands of a trusted officer, Thomas Crawford of Jordanhill, and in the early hours of 1 April, 1571, Crawford, with his guide and a hundred of his best men, began to scale the treacherous heights. Before dawn had broken over the great fortress the scaling party clambered over the battlements and launched themselves at their astonished enemies. Fierce fighting ensued but surprise and boldness won the day and by noon Lennox himself was able to ride into the castle at the head of his cheering troops.

Thomas Crawford later became a Provost of Glasgow and is credited for having saved the Cathedral from the hands of the Reformers. He didn't mind them 'dingin doon the High Kirk' he said just as long as they were willing to build a new one first!

THE SARACEN'S HEAD INN

THE GRAND OPENING of the Saracen's Head Inn was announced in the *Glasgow Journal,* and among the attractions listed were 36 rooms whose beds were guaranteed 'good, clean, and free from bugs'. A proud boast in the year 1755!

Glasgow had never before had a proper hotel and the magistrates gave Robert Tennent every encouragement in his enterprise, selling him land cheaply and supplying the building materials free.

The ground on which the inn was erected had formerly been occupied by the church of Little Saint Mungo, and the stonework used in the building was taken from the ruins of the Bishop's Palace. Not many inns in Scotland could claim such a religious background.

Supplying the best of food and drink the inn became the centre of the city's social life, and young ladies would pay five shillings for the privilege of standing in the spacious kitchen and observing the preparation and presentation of exotic and sumptuous meals.

No journey to Glasgow was complete without a visit to the inn, and every visitor of note was sure to make an appearance there. Dr Johnson, Burns, Scott, Wordsworth all dined and drank in the Saracen's Head.

With stable accommodation for 60 horses, the inn quickly became the chief coaching station in the city, and in 1788 the first London mail coach duly arrived, accompanied by an army of trumpet-blowing, musket-firing horsemen. It was a joyous day as the cavalcade thundered in along the Gallowgate, ushering in another advance in Glasgow's longed-for progress towards national recognition and importance.

MARKET DAY

IN THE EARLY YEARS of the 19th century when farmers and other country folk poured into Glasgow on the traditional Wednesday market day, the area around Stockwell Street and the Trongate would become a seething mass of livestock and humanity.

Horses and hens, cows and pigs, ducks and geese ... would all add to the general clamour as countrymen and townsfolk argued and bargained over the merits and value of animals and produce.

Farmers' children guzzled on delectable dainties purchased at the sweetie-wives' stalls, and country girls seeking employment paraded the streets hoping to catch the eye of prospective employers, while fighting off the advances of amorous 'townies'.

Hawkers and beggars, conmen and thieves, clerics and scholars ... all were to be found enjoying this, the high spot of the city's week.

And if the townsfolk enjoyed it, the countryfolk loved it. Whether they made a profit or loss they would still have something to talk about in the quiet country days ahead, of how they had – 'outsmarted' some city slicker ... or had been 'cheated' by another.

If they were lucky they would find Hawkie or Jamie Blue there to regale them with story, poem, or ballad. Hawkie, their favourite, would be plied with buttermilk and enjoined to tell a joke or two. He always would, provided his country cousins would first of all remove their headgear 'as it's no' the fashion in this toon tae put hats on cabbage stalks'.

And when the last weary farmer had left for home counting his profit, or his unsold livestock, then the city would be handed back to its natural dwellers, and all that remained of the weekly rural invasion would be a little breath of country air ... and a great deal of country fertiliser.

FIRE!

ON A HOT JUNE DAY in 1652, a fire broke out in an alleyway above Glasgow Cross. Flying sparks landed on the thatched roofs of nearby houses and soon the flames were sweeping irresistibly along the Trongate, Saltmarket, and Bridgegate.

People rushed into the streets with their belongings in a desperate attempt to salvage something from the holocaust, but by now the very air seemed to be on fire, and the pathetic bundles of clothing stacked in the narrow streets burst into fires of their own.

It was the most devastating misfortune ever to have befallen Glasgow, with a third of the town destroyed and more than a thousand families homeless. Small wonder the town council declared that 'unless speedy remedy be used, the town shall come to utter ruin.'

Parliament donated £1000 towards a relief fund, and collections were made in churches throughout the land. Even Cromwell assisted by foregoing the monthly levy imposed for the upkeep of his army of occupation.

A SECOND GREAT FIRE in 1677 emphasised the folly of narrow streets lined with wooden, straw-thatched houses, and new building regulations were introduced that were to change the face of the city. In years to come Glasgow was to be praised for its handsome stone buildings and clear, wide streets. Daniel Defoe, author of *Robinson Crusoe*, and inveterate traveller, declared Glasgow to be without doubt 'the most beautiful little town in Europe'.

PLAGUE!

IN 1588 THE CITIZENS of Glasgow were forbidden, under heavy penalty, from trading with the good people of Paisley and Kilmacolm. The reason was that Paisley and Kilmacolm had plague. Glasgow hadn't.

But in 1647 it had. The epidemic reached such proportions that masters and students of the University fled the city and settled in the relative safety of Irvine. Many of the less fortunate stayed behind and died.

Like all medieval communities, Glasgow was the victim of diseases it didn't understand and had no way of combating. Leprosy was the most dreaded. A law provided for the sustenance of lepers in a proper place outwith the Burgh'. That 'proper place' was ordained to be in Saint Ninian's Leper Hospital in the village of Brigend, situated on the south side of the Old Bridge. The site of the hospital came to be known as Hospital Street, and Brigend was, of course, the cluster of houses later to be known as Gorbals.

On two days a week the afflicted lepers were allowed to enter Glasgow provided they covered their faces with muslin, walked in the middle of the roadway, and sounded clappers to warn people of their coming.

In later years typhus and cholera were to become the scourge of the people, with every new attack claiming thousands of lives until improved sanitation and the Loch Katrine water supply helped to eradicate the diseases.

THE BRAVE MRS BELLAMY

IN 1764 MRS GEORGE ANN BELLAMY, darling of the London and Edinburgh stage, agreed to become the darling of the Glasgow stage. There was one slight problem – Glasgow didn't have a stage for her to be the darling of!

With most people in Glasgow regarding the stage as nothing less than the 'Temple of Satan' it was found to be impossible to purchase land on which to build a theatre, and it was eventually built outside the burgh, in the village of Grahamston, now the site of Central Station.

On the night before the grand opening a fiery Methodist preacher led an angry mob from the Trongate to the new theatre where stage, scenery, and costumes, were duly set alight. The theatre itself somehow managed to survive the blaze.

Mrs Bellamy entered town the next day and was told of the fire that had surely put paid to her Glasgow debut. But she wasn't daunted, the famous actress ordered the word to be spread throughout town that she would indeed appear and act at the theatre that very night.

Her courage won the admiration of many of the city's more civilised and cosmopolitan citizens, and in a surge of civic pride and dynamic determination a makeshift stage was hastily erected, and scenery was painted, while costumes were donated by the ladies of the town. The play was performed on schedule and acclaimed a great success.

Success or not, the fact remains that for her own safety Mrs Bellamy had to be escorted back to her lodgings at the Black Bull Inn by a company of the Town Guard.

The theatre had arrived in Glasgow – but only just!

GLASGOW'S TRAMS

IT WAS IN 1894 that Glasgow Corporation took upon itself the task of providing transport for its citizens. Until then the job had been done by private concerns, mainly the Glasgow Tramway and Omnibus Company, managed by Andrew Menzies and operating 40 horse drawn services throughout the city.

The Corporation took over the Tramway and Omnibus Company and immediately began a programne of improvement and expansion. Before long it found itself employing 3500 horses that were pulling 54 million passengers a year.

The new system was so successful, and so profitable, that it was soon able to reduce fares by half. It was also able to boast that on most routes 'at least one tram will always be in sight'.

In 1902 electrification was introduced, and the golden age of the Glasgow tramcar began. By 1930 the system was carrying 500 million paying customers a year, and was the envy of cities the world over.

Times, however, changed, and as more and more vehicles appeared on the streets of the city the tram car came to be blamed for much of the congestion. A programme of contraction and phasing-out was introduced, and in 1962 the last tram ran between Dalmuir West and Auchenshuggle.

GLASGOW'S WATER

MUSIC PLAYED, cannons roared, thousands cheered ... and 50 million gallons of Loch Katrine water began the daily, downward plunge to slake the thirst and wash the dirty faces of half a million Glaswegians.

On 14 October, 1859, Queen Victoria pulled the handle that opened the sluice and sent the precious liquid tumbling on its 34-mile journey towards the factories, the mills, and the people of the ever-growing city.

What a change from 60 years before, when the only supply of water was to be found in the city's public wells.

IN 1804 WILLIAM HARLEY had improved matters by erecting a reservoir at the head of West Nile Street and selling the water in the city streets at a halfpenny a stoupful (pailful). It was a lucrative enterprise, with profits running at £4000 per annum.

But still the city cried out for more water, and in 1806 the Glasgow Water Works Company was formed and began a supply of filtered water from the Clyde. Years later the Cranstonhill Water Works Company came into operation.

After their amalgamation in 1838, many new schemes to increase the intake of water was proposed, begun, and then abandoned, until finally the Corporation of Glasgow took over and began the mammoth task of bringing the waters of Loch Katrine to the people of the city.

BONNIE PRINCE CHARLIE

FRAMED in the window of the Shawfield Mansion in the Trongate could be seen the resplendent figure of a solitary diner. A handsome man, dressed in fine silk tartan, he dined daily in full view of anyone caring to look.

In the Glasgow of 1745 very few did.

Four times he appeared in the city streets 'without acclamation or a single huzza'. No bells were rung and no respect paid him by even the meanest inhabitant. He asked for recruits to join him in the fight against the English and a drunken shoemaker joined his ranks.

'Our very ladies had not the curiosity to go near him,' said Provost Andrew Cochrane. But one lady did, and when the beautiful Clementina Walkinshaw set eyes on Prince Charles Edward Stuart she gave her heart and soul to him.

When 'Bonnie Prince Charlie' lost his war against the English the news was received in Glasgow with bonfires and great rejoicing. Charles fled to the safety of France and sent for Clementina to join him there, and the daughter of the Laird of Camlachie and Barrowfield fled to his side.

She was named Countess of Alberstrof by the King of France, and in 1753 she bore a daughter to the Prince. Charlotte, her daughter, became the Duchess of Albany and her beauty was praised by Robert Burns in *The Bonnie Lass of Albany*.

Bonnie Prince Charlie died in Rome in 1788, and Charlotte, Duchess of Albany died the following year.

Clementina Walkinshaw, the Glasgow girl who stole the heart of the Young Chevalier, died in 1802 at Fribourg, in Switzerland.

WOLFE OF QUEBEC
– AND GLASGOW!

CUMBERLAND THE BUTCHER smiled thinly as he looked around the bloody field of Culloden. Dead and dying Highlanders lay everywhere, and the sight was sweet to Cumberland's eye. Ahead of him a wounded Scot crawled towards a boulder, attempting to escape the systematic slaughter of the survivors of Bonnie Prince Charlie's tragic army.

'Finish him,' the Butcher told the young officer at his side. Major James Wolfe, one of Cumberland's finest soldiers and the man destined to pave the way towards the conquest of Canada for England, refused.

The decision to have nothing to do with the murderous blood-letting of Culloden seemed to be typical of the high ideals and sense of honour of Wolfe of Quebec.

THREE YEARS LATER Wolfe was stationed in Glasgow where his impeccable manners and friendly nature made him a favourite of those citizens who enjoyed the honour of hosting the officers of the King's Army.

How were they to know that the gentle, courteous officer whose company they vied for, and paraded their unmarried daughters in front of, was describing them in a letter to a soldier friend in the following savage words: 'The men here are civil, designing, and treacherous – the women cold, coarse, and cunning.' There was it seems, after all, a wolf in Wolfe's clothing!

MARY QUEEN OF SCOTS

WHEN MARY QUEEN OF SCOTS finally escaped from the island fortress in Loch Leven an event was set in motion that 'settled the fate of Scotland, affected the future of England, and had its influence over all Europe.' The event was, of course, the Battle of Langside.

With her liberty restored 'to the astonishment of everyone', Mary set forth for Dumbarton Castle, heading an army sworn to united action in her name. In Glasgow, the news of Mary's advance was received by Regent Moray, who immediately assembled an army to block the Queen's way. The spot he chose to meet her was Langside Hill.

On 13 May, 1568, with Mary watching from the safety of a nearby hill, the two armies joined battle. Cannons roared, cavalry charged, and pikemen met in fierce hand to hand fighting that raged through the narrow streets and tiny gardens of Langside Village.

Marksmen, placed behind dykes and hedgerows by the Regent Moray, directed a withering fire into the side of the Queen's army, while the Laird of Grange, Moray's trusted general, returned with additional troops and attacked their flank.

The Queen's army broke and fled from the field of battle, leaving behind their dead, their dying – and their young Queen's dream of the Throne of Scotland.

OLIVER CROMWELL

ON 3 SEPTEMBER, 1650, Oliver Cromwell and his army of 16000 men stood with the North Sea behind them and a Scottish army of almost 30,000 before them. Disaster seemed inevitable. The Scots had merely to hold their position and victory must surely be theirs. Unknown to Cromwell, however, the Scots general, Leslie, was being badgered and bullied by clergymen following the Presbyterian army to sweep down and 'slay the Philistines'.

Seeing the Scots advance from their unassailable stronghold, Cromwell raised his hands to heaven and cried 'Praised be the Lord! He hath delivered them into the hands of his servant.' The Scots were put to flight with thousands slain or taken prisoner and the way to Edinburgh and Glasgow was open.

Arriving in Glasgow, Cromwell set about winning friends and influencing people, and despite being at the receiving end of a public lecture from the Reverend Zachary Boyd in the Cathedral – during which an officer begged permission from Cromwell to 'pistol the old scoundrel' – Cromwell invited the fiery minister to dine with him.

When the meal was over, Cromwell concluded the evening with a prayer reputed to be almost three hours long and which sent the Reverend Boyd home feeling that his host was, perhaps, not quite so bad a fellow as he had been led to believe.

WILLIAM WALLACE

IN THE YEAR 1300, William Wallace entered Glasgow at the head of a squadron of cavalry and set in motion what was to become known as the Battle of the Bell o' the Brae. This was the name given to what was then the steepest part of the High Street, and it was here that Wallace met the army of Earl Percy, champion of Edward I of England, and destroyer of military forces in western Scotland.

Convinced that Percy would choose the Bell o' the Brae on which to meet him, Wallace divided his force and sent the Laird of Auchinleck on a route that would lead him up the Drygate and behind Percy. The Scottish patriot then led his remaining troops into the High Street and there, to his great relief found himself facing the English invaders.

Fierce fighting commenced as the Scottish horsemen hurled themselves into the midst of the enemy, their swords and battle-axes cutting a bloody path before them, and it was at this precise moment that Auchinleck and the other Scots came charging into the rear of Percy's bewildered force.

As the English troops broke in confusion Wallace caught sight of the redoubtable Percy. Urging his horse forward he drew level with his opponent and, legend says, with one stroke of his fearsome broadsword 'cleft Percy's head in two'. The English retreat became a rout, and Wallace was left in command of the field of battle.

KEEPER OF GLASGOW'S CATTLE

JOHN TEMPLETOUN LEFT his cottage in Glasgow Green and made his unhurried way to the town cross. Arriving there he drew his breath, raised his cowhorn to his lips, and blew. The long, mournful bellow rolled through the early morning mist and along the walls of the straw-thatched cottages lining the High Street and Gallowgate. Another blow and once more the silent streets echoed the old, primitive sound. Glasgow's town-herd was calling his charges to order.

From barn and byre, from garden and gatepost, cattle would be turned free to answer the call of John's horn, their eager hooves sinking deep into the mud and mire of the rutted pathways.

With his stick to prod and his horn to beguile, the town-herd would lead the cows through the West Port and into the open country beyond Stockwell. From there he would follow the path trodden by countless others before him, along the Trongate, up the Cow Loan (Queen Street) then over to the pasture land at the village of Cowcaddens.

There, in the lush green fields of the common grazing, the town's cattle would eat their fill of grass and them, by their own special magic, convert it into foaming milk to slake the thirst of Glasgow's growing population.

CHAPTER 16

Foreign Parts: Partick and Govan

THE DRUNK MAN stood outside the Bridgend Inn of Partick and tried to remember what he had been doing before entering the inn some four hours earlier. It had been something important, he knew. But what?

He shook his head in a vain attempt to clear the alcoholic haze that clouded his memory, then staggered forward a pace or two before falling over a drum that some fool had left lying in the middle of the road.

And then he remembered ... it was his drum. For he was Sandy Stewart, the man whose job it was to drum the villagers to bed at nine o' clock each night, then rouse them eight hours later and set them off on another days work.

Hanging the drum around his neck he found his drumsticks and began where he had left off – beating the nine o'clock drum. The only trouble was that it was now one o'clock in the morning.

Soon there was a stream of tired workers heading for the Pointhouse Ferry and a six o'clock start at the silk works in Govan. Only when the enraged ferryman was roused from his sleep was the real time discovered.

As the incensed workers made their way back home in the dark,, they discussed what form the impending retribution to be meted out on the village drummer would take.

When five o'clock came, Sandy and his drum were locked in the arms of a deep and peaceful slumber induced by an overindulgence of spirits and a self-righteous satisfaction in a job well done. It is said that the whole of Partick slept in that morning.

Sandy Stewart wasn't alone in enjoying the delights of the local hostelries, for it was noted in 1823 that while the village had neither church nor mission-hall it did have seven ale-houses. According to the minister of Govan parish 'their pestiferous effects on the health and virtuous habits of the people were only too apparent'.

And it wasn't only the inhabitants of Partick who were drawn to the inns and ale-houses. From Glasgow, too, came happy bands of weekend strollers, enjoying the country air and the sylvan scenes around the sprawling village that straddled the clear, cascading waters of the River Kelvin. The ale of Partick never tasted sweeter than after the long walk from Glasgow.

And then there were the ducks! The old 'Bun and Ale Inn' enjoyed such a reputation for roast duck that it became the home of the Duck Club of Partick, a fraternity of Glasgow businessmen who travelled through each Saturday to be fed the most succulent, superior duck imaginable. Redolent with sage and onion, served with Partick peas, it was a feast fit for kings.

The most enthusiastic member of the Duck Club of Partick was one William McTear, convener of the Glasgow Incorporation of Cordiners. So prodigious was Willie's appetite for Partick Duck, so insatiable his desire, that children were known to run before him singing:

The ducks of Partick quack with fear,
Crying, Lord preserve us! Here's McTear!

There were, of course, other villages on the outskirts of Glasgow. In 1578 Bishop Leslie had written his History of Scotland and duly noted that 'twa myles alone the toune of Renfrou is a gret and large village named Goeuan ... it's ale is wondrous good.'

The ale of 'Goeuan' (Govan) must have been wondrous good indeed, for according to tradition no less a personage than King James V of Scotland was wont to drop into the Ferrie Bot Inn at Water Row and spend a happy day or two sampling the landlord's brew. If it was good enough for the King then it was certainly good enough for the people of the village whose fondness for it caused the kirk session many a troubled time. The session records bear testimony to the number of parishioners who were 'rebookit and exhorted to refrain from such lyke drunkiness in tyme coming.'

Years later another historian was to complain that as far as the villagers of Govan were concerned 'temperance has not obtained a place among the cardinal virtues'.

And it wasn't only the adult population who caused concern. On 2 April, 1652, it was noted that 'Ye bairnes of Particke are verie much given to swearing and prophaning the Lord's Day by playing in tyme of sermone.' Two weeks later the Govan ferryman, Andro Cochrane appeared before the kirk session accused of transporting people 'over ye water on ye Lord's Day'. Andro denied the charge and claimed that the people referred to 'took ye bot in his absence.'

In 1711 the congregation were still being 'rebookit', only then it was for 'gazing out of doors and windows unnecessarily'. But if the members of the kirk session were sometimes hard on their wayward brethren they were also aware of the needs of their less fortunate fellows, for it is recorded that 'Robert Mure, elder, should buy a byble for the poore damsell named Bessie Shiels', and that 30 shillings should be given to James Will 'for having sustained a great loss of his cattel to a wood dog (wolf?), and for having eight children.'

Whether or not it was a wolf that decimated the cattle of James Will we'll never know – but we do know what happened to the flock of sheep that belonged to a minister of the Govan parish many, many years ago.

The story began, we're told, with a young man leading his bride-to-be to the shallow reaches of the River Clyde and bidding her cross over and wait for him on the other side. There was business to be attended to before leaving forever the village where he had suffered great indignity from his lover's employer, the minister of the parish.

It had been opposition from the minister that had forced them to steal away like thieves in the night. Now was the time for revenge. Through the sleeping village and over fields heavy with dew, the groom made his way towards the manse. In his hand he clutched a dagger whose large and fearful blade he had honed to razor sharpness. Reaching the field wherein the minister grazed his flock of sheep he set about avenging the wrongs done to him. One by one the terrified sheep were chased, caught, stabbed and beheaded. Only when the last head had been severed did the young man hurry away to join his waiting lover, pausing only to wash the reeking blood from his hands in the cool crystal waters of the gurgling river. When dawn eventually broke at last the news of the slaughter spread like wildfire through the entire village. Everyone had known of the minister's fierce opposition and of his many attempts to keep the boy and girl apart. How would they react to this terrible and bloody revenge? They reacted by picking the largest and finest of the sheep's heads and parading it through the village streets atop a gaily coloured pole.

And they did so for many years, at the annual Govan fair on the first Friday of every June.

BUT NOT EVEN the ancient Govan Fair could surpass the excitement, the crowds, and the pure unalloyed pleasure of the events of Saturday, 27 June, 1885.

Govan had never seen anything like it. From the entrance to the Burgh at Paisley Road Toll, and as far as the eye could see, the air was thick with flags and bunting of every size, shape, and colour. The laughing, shouting Govanites thronged in the streets, their numbers swollen by a massive surge of strangers and visitors come to see the celebrations, listen to the speeches, and follow the marching, playing bands.

In the unlikely event that anyone was unaware of the reason for the celebrations there were clues aplenty in the banners proclaiming 'All honour to Mrs Elder, her name shall live forever' and 'Mrs Elder, future generations shall rise and bless your name.'

The Burgh was about to take possession of a gift that, even more than a century later, continues to provide much pleasure. The gift was, of course, Elder Park. Donated by Mrs Elder in loving memory of her famous father-in-law, David, and her even more famous husband, John Elder, who was founder of the Fairfield Shipbuilding Company, and employer of many of the thousands who celebrated this historic day, the park was to provide a green oasis where parents and children could find peace and relaxation from the busy workaday world of shipyards and bustling tenements.

Small wonder that the Indian Tea Bazaar in Govan Road should proudly proclaim:

'With Elder Park and Bazaar Tea, Govan now content should be.'

And Govan was indeed content.

CHAPTER 17

TheResurrection of Mathew Clydesdale

THERE ARE MANY strange stories concerning the public executions of criminals that once took place in the streets of Glasgow – Andrew Marshall, with the hangman's noose around his neck, leaping upwards to grasp the gallows arm, while the city executioner beat furiously upon his desperately clutching hands with a hastily snatched piece of wood or Lord Provost John Dunlop in 1798 pushing the nervous, fumbling official hangman aside and pulling the bolt which sent murderer John McMillan plunging into eternity. But of all the public executions that took place in Glasgow that of Mathew Clydesdale deserves special mention – not for what happened on the gallows, but for what was said to have happened afterwards.

It is a story almost beyond belief – and indeed, there are grounds for believing that the most sensational part of the story took place only in the vivid, and flawed, imagination of Peter McKenzie, the man whose eyewitness account of the whole affair has been seized joyfully, and elaborated upon extensively, by city historians ever since.

The story begins in the realms of fact and authenticated detail. It is a fact that on 27 August, 1818, Mathew Clydesdale, 'an athletic and extremly muscular man', in a drunken rage beat to death 80-year-old Alexander Love.

There appeared to be no particular reason for this violent act – no more reason than there was for his having thrown the family cat onto the fire that same day, as a witness was to testify. At the trial on 3 October, 1818, presided over by Lords Gillies and Succoth, the jury lost no time in finding Clydesdale guilty of the murder of the old man. Clydesdale 'of ferocious countenance' showed no surprise at the outcome of the trial, and no emotion at being sentenced to public execution in front of the jail at Glasgow Green.

What did surprise and shock him was the fact that Lord Gillies also decreed that he should be fed nothing but bread and water, and that after his death his body should be delivered up to Dr James Jeffray, Professor of Anatomy at Glasgow University, 'there to be publicly dissected and anatomised'.

This savage punishment was designed to serve two purposes: to provide the city anatomists with 'fresh and healthy' cadavers, and to dissuade potential criminals from a life of crime, it being then widely believed that the soul of a dismembered corpse could not present itself before the Gates of Heaven.

While awaiting execution, Clydesdale, held prisoner in the Tolbooth, in the throes of despair and dread, attempted suicide by slashing his arms with a broken bottle. His frantic jailers sent for Dr Corkindale, the prison surgeon, who staunched the flowing blood, dressed the wounds, and saved the wretched prisoner for the hangman.

And so, on 4 November, 1818, before thousands of curious Glaswegians, and guarded by the 40th Regiment of Foot and a detachment of the First Dragoon Guards, Mathew Clydesdale was duly hanged. At four pm his body was removed from the gallows, placed in a wooden box, then taken by an open horse-drawn cart up the High Street to the University and Dr Jeffray. In the Anatomy Hall of the University the lifeless body of Clydesdale was placed in a chair and a bizarre series of experiments involving a Galvanic battery (used to administer chemically produced electric shocks) was begun before the wondering eyes of students, teachers, visitors ... and Peter McKenzie.

What follows is a necessarily condensed version of McKenzie's eyewitness account of the experiments, as described in Volume 2 of his *Reminiscences of Glasgow*.

'A light air tube, connected with the galvanic battery, was soon placed in one of his nostrils. The bellows began to blow in that nostril in solemn reality. His chest immediately heaved! He drew breath!

A few more operations went swiftly on – which really we cannot very well describe – but at last the tongue of the murderer moved out of his lips, his eyes now opened widely – he stared, apparently in astonishment, around him; while his head, arms and legs actually moved; and we declare he made a feeble attempt as if to rise from the chair whereon he was seated.

He did positively rise from it in a moment or two afterwards, and stood upright; at seeing which a thrill ran through the excited and crowded room ... that he had now actually come to life again through the extraordinary operation of the galvanic battery!

At this most sudden, startling, and unexpected sight, some of the students screamed out in horror; not a few of them fainted on the spot ... and ere the lapse of another minute or two Dr Jeffray pulled out his unerring lancet and plunged it into the jugular vein of the culprit, who instantly fell down upon the floor like a slaughtered ox on the blow of the butcher.'

If this really was the scene, and the events witnessed by McKenzie are as described, then what nightmare, what vision of hell did Clydesdale imagine the Anatomy Hall to be, as he stood like Frankenstein's monster with wires and tubes dangling from his poor, abused body?

In nine weeks he had committed murder, attempted suicide, been executed, and now (according to McKenzie) been resurrected – then promptly executed once again. How sweet true death would have seemed to him.

But were the experiments of that day – and their results – really and truly as McKenzie remembered and described them? Or was his earlier comment – 'a few more experiments went swiftly on, which really we cannot very well describe' – all too true?

The 'few more experiments' that McKenzie was unable, or unwilling, to describe included the body of Clydesdale being 'well nigh drained of blood' ... incisions being made in various parts of the body, including the neck, chest, hip, heel, fingers, forehead ... and a section of the Atlas vertebra (supporting the skull) being removed, revealing the spinal column.

These incisions and removals performed by Mr Marshall, assistant to Dr Jeffray, took place before those that were described by McKenzie. Under these circumstances it seems obvious that more than a galvanic battery would have been required to bring Clydesdale to his feet.

What the power of the galvanic battery, owned and operated by Dr Andrew Ure, would have done, when brought into contact with the various exposed nerves of the bloodless, lifeless corpse seated on the Anatomy Hall stage, was cause dead limbs and dead muscles to twitch, twist, contort and convulse.

Dead fingers moved and seemed to point to members of the audience, some of whom fled the room in terror. One man fainted as Clydesdale's face seemed to smile, then frown, then scowl angrily as electric rods were pushed under the incised flap of skin on his forehead and activated the 'supra-orbital' nerve. A dead leg shot forward with such force that it almost knocked over one of the assistants, while in another experiment heavy breathing was induced ... but stopped the instant the battery was disconnected from the body.

Despite the vivid imaginings of Peter McKenzie, Mathew Clydesdale never stood up in the Anatomy Hall of Glasgow University, and Professor Jeffray never 'plunged his unerring lancet into his jugular vein' as a means of finally killing off the wretched Clydesdale.

He never spoke and he didn't bleed as later recorded by some, who really should have known better.

The nearest Mathew Clydesdale came to being resurrected was in the thoughtful comment made by Dr Ure in his 'Account of Experiments on the Body of a Criminal after Execution', published in *The Journal of Science and Arts*, 1819: 'In deliberating on the above galvanic phenomena, we are almost willing to imagine that if, without cutting into and wounding the spinal marrow and blood vessels in the neck, the pulmonary organs had been set a-playing at first by electrifying the phrenic nerve [as proposed by Dr Ure but overruled by Professor Jeffray] there is a probability that life might have been restored.'

In short, Dr Ure is suggesting that had the body not been drained of blood, and had the spinal cord not been severed, and had part of the vertebra not been removed, and had the body not been incised in numerous places, then, and only then, he could 'almost imagine' the restoration of life. This is a far cry from Peter McKenzie's eye witness account of the new 'Resurrection', his confident assertion that '[Clydesdale] had now actually come to life again' – and it is a million long and lurid miles from the more sensational and bloodthirsty accounts that were to follow. So why, from his privileged point of view, and with all this documented information so readily available, did McKenzie get it so wrong and mislead so many others that were to follow?

He was 19 years of age when he saw the experiments take place, and 67 years of age when Volume Two of his *Reminiscences of Glasgow* was published. Forty-six years is a long time to hold on to a memory, even one as horrific and spectacular as this. This version of these events certainly make for a better story than Dr Ure's staid and scientific version and Peter McKenzie liked a good story, even if his telling of it was, as described in *Memoirs and Portraits of One Hundred Glasgow Men* – 'very often slapdash and slipshod'.

But perhaps there is some tiny shred of justification for Dr Ure believing that if the body in question had not suffered so much under the surgeon's knife before the commencement of the galvanic experiments, then it could indeed have been restored to life ...

In 1818, the year in which Clydesdale was hanged, the 'long drop' in which a murderer's neck is broken was not in vogue, and death was most often caused by slow strangulation. It had been noted during the execution that while Clydesdale had appeared to die almost immediately, Simon Ross, hanged at the same time and on the same gallows, had died only after a fierce and convulsive struggle. It was also noted by Dr Ure that when Clydesdale's body was brought into the anatomy hall, 'His face had a perfectly natural aspect, being neither livid nor tumified and there was no dislocation of his neck.'

Was it possible that the unfortunate Clydesdale had been suffocated into a deep coma and could perhaps have been shocked out of it by an earlier and more judicious application of the galvanic battery? If so, then it was an episode which casts no credit on the city's judicial system, on the University and its teachers ... or on the work of Tam Young, the city hangman.

CHAPTER 18

Let Glasgow Flourish

IN 1975 Glasgow celebrated the 800th anniversary of its establishment as a burgh. To fully understand the importance of Bishop Jocelyn's gaining burgh status for his people, and its consequent effect upon the growth and development of the city, it is necessary to look beyond the recorded history of the region and back to the first bishop, Kentigern.

In the sixth century, Kentigern founded a church and a thriving community of priests and converts on the banks of the Molendinar, a community that he must have felt would grow and flourish after he had gone, but which instead fell into decay as his followers fled from the heathen tribes who took possession of the land.

Not until the early part of the 12th century does a clear picture of Glasgow reappear, when King David I reconstituted the bishopric, appointed John Achaius bishop, and made Glasgow the centre of the church in the west of Scotland. The establishment of the bishop and his court provided a timely stimulus, and over the years there was a gradual increase in population as traders and craftsmen set up in business under the kindly protection of succeeding bishops. Stretching from the cathedral down to the Clyde, the little town reached a critical point in its development. Bound by the law of the land to do their trading in the royal burghs of Dumbarton and Rutherglen, the merchants of the town were restricted in their progress and hampered by the tolls and customs imposed upon their goods and produce.

Jocelyn decided that the time was ripe for change. Overtures were made to William the Lion, King of Scotland, and in 1175 Glasgow became a Burgh of Barony, entitled to hold her own market on Thursdays and to collect tolls and market dues from all the goods entering the town.

Jocelyn became the ruler of Glasgow and all lands surrounding it. He had the power of life and death over its citizens, the right to collect taxes, and the authority to elect bailies and town officers. His power was used wisely and the new burgh began to prosper. Gates were erected at the four entrances to the town and served the dual role of making easier the collection of tolls and customs, as well as stopping of strangers in time of war and pestilence.

Despite the fierce opposition from Dumbarton and Rutherglen, who found themselves losing both money and trade to the Glaswegian upstarts, the town continued to prosper and by the mid-16th century had become the richest burgh on the Clyde, boasting among its possessions a cathedral, a castle, and a university.

The area around the cathedral bristled with the great houses of the clergy, while the lower part of town bustled with lively industry as salmon fishers, herring curers, tanners, weavers, and coopers went about their business. Bishop Rae's bridge across the Clyde was a scene of continuous activity as farmers and other country folk brought their produce into town for sale, with the customs officers taking a ladleful of grain from each sack, and a handful of wool from each bale brought forward. The revenue thus collected would be used to maintain and improve the running of the town.

It was, by and large, a happy and peaceful time. The 17th century was less kind, however, and there was a long period when it seemed that the limit of expansion had been reached.

The Act of Union brought a new burst of activity as trade with the English colonies in North America was opened up to Glasgow's merchants. So well did they grasp the opportunity that by 1750 half the tobacco entering Britain found its way into the warehouses of the Clyde. Great wealth was accumulated by the 'Tobacco Lords' and many fine mansions were built by this new aristocracy. Glasgow was now the chief commercial city of Scotland, and soon to be on the brink of its greatest period of expansion.

When the American War of Independence brought the tobacco trade to an end, Glasgow's merchants turned with determination and vigour to cotton, then later to the newer industries involving coal, iron, and shipping. The little market town of yesteryear was preparing to become the industrial giant of the future, and the second city of the British Empire.

The story of Glasgow from the 12th to the 20th century had been one of gradual progression and expansion. Since 1975 the city has been in a turmoil of contraction and change. Large numbers of the population have moved to new towns, and whole districts have vanished to make way for motorways and multi-storey flats. Links with the early past are fast disappearing and can only be seen in the handful of buildings still left untouched by the planners and the ever-active demolishers.

It would seem that the city's ties with the past are to be found more in the traditions and customs handed down to us by our industrious and far-sighted forefathers, the men whose ambitions and pride demanded equality as a burgh ... whose versatility and business acumen allowed them to seize on every opportunity and innovation ... whose faith in their city caused them not to move mountains, but to transform the sleepy Clyde into an ocean highway that was to reach out and declare itself on every sea and in every port.

What the next 800 years hold we cannot say, but the city is changing to meet the challenge – and while Glasgow changes, Glasgow lives.